K A R M A

The Definitive Guide to the Supreme Law of this World

RICHARD ANDREW KING

Published by Richard King Publications
PO Box 3621
Laguna Hills, CA 92654
(www.RichardKing.net)

Library of Congress Cataloging-in-Publication Data
King, Richard Andrew
Karma – The Definitive Guide to the Supreme Law of this World
ISBN: 978-0-931872-00-6; Price: 9000
Date of Publication: 28 April 2019

DEDICATION

To MCSJ for his illimitable, unfathomable

and eternal Love, Grace and Guidance.

ACKNOWLEDGEMENTS

A special thanks to Liana Moisescu

for her beautiful and artistic

book cover design talents.

http://lianadesigns.crevado.com/

https://99designs.com/profiles/1544664

Richard Andrew King

CONTACT

Richard Andrew King

PO Box 3621, Laguna Hills, CA 92654-3621

RichardKing.net | Rich@RichardKing.net

KARMA

The Definitive Guide to the Supreme Law of this World

TABLE OF CONTENTS

Richard Andrew King

AUTHOR'S PREFACE

Karma is a universally known concept throughout the world. Simultaneously, however, the argument can be made that karma is also universally misunderstood. This book is designed to shed light on the reality that karma is not just a simple word that can be bandied about with abandon but, rather, that karma is the Supreme Law of this creation.

The higher purpose of this work is to share ideas of karma relative to the expansion of one's spiritual life and the ascent of the soul beyond the borders of this material dimension and into higher realms of consciousness, the ultimate culmination being God Realization, i.e., the merging of our soul with that of the Creator.

The provenance of the core of the information given here is from Saints such as Namdev, Rumi, Kabir, Ravidas, Nanak, Tukaram, Dariya of Bihar, Dadu, Tulsi Sahib, Swami Ji, Baba Ji Maharaj, Sawan Singh, Jagat Singh, Charan Singh, Buddha and the Bible. These esteemed souls are the apotheosis of Spiritual and Mystical knowledge, knowledge which is openly available for all seekers of Truth but not promoted extensively as one would promote material/carnal products and endeavors for worldly consumption.

Richard Andrew King

Verily, the information shared by Saints and Mystics is powerful. It can not only change people's lives but revolutionize their existence. This author has found no higher teachings in this world than those of Saints.

There is a constant drumbeat in this book from beginning to end, which is by design. That drumbeat is this:

We sow; we reap and we cannot reap what we do not sow.

This phrase expresses a simple law which is not just a thought but actually *the* Law of this creation. It is hard to live by Karmic Law but nonetheless imperative for our well being. Furthermore, we are bound by and to Karmic Law, for it is immutable and inescapable and applies to every living being, to every life in this creation.

With peaceful and harmonious blessings,

Richard Andrew King

CHAPTER ONE

THE SUPREME LAW

KARMA is the Supreme, Eternal, Universal, Immutable, Irrefutable, Inescapable, Inviolable, Irrevocable, Inexorable, Self-Operating **LAW** of this Creation. Simply defined, karma is the process of action and reaction, cause and effect, choice and consequence, sowing and reaping.

There is a notion that karma refers only to those actions that are negative or seen as bad. Actually, karma references all acts whether they're bad or good. Karma is simply the Sanskrit word describing the process of action and reaction. Hateful or destructive actions yield reactions of the same type. Loving or positive actions generate reactions that match their energy. Whatever we put onto the circle of life – positive or negative – circles back to encircle us. This is Karmic Law. Yet, it is incredibly stunning how the most universal and fundamental law of this creation is so universally and fundamentally ignored.

Karma has no conscience. Furthermore, we don't get to choose whether we're affected by Karmic Law or not. No mortal is powerful enough, bright enough or deceptive enough to manipulate Karmic Law. We are bound by it, bound to it. It plays no favorites. No king, queen, prince, princess, pop star, rock star, movie star, sports star, millionaire, billionaire, trillionaire, celebrity, president, pauper, pope, potentate, priest, minister, doctor, lawyer, educator, judge, janitor, maid, man, woman, child, human, animal, bird, fish, insect or plant escapes it, ever! Karma is the King of Laws in this world.

Says Saint Charan Singh: (*Quest for Light*, 3rd edition, 1977, RSSB, p.394)

Every one, including animals, birds and even plants has its own karmas to go through. The Law of Karma is working relentlessly in this world and all are reaping what they sowed in the past.

Karma acts with impunity and immunity from all living things or beings in this creation. Karma is *the* Supreme Law of this world.

Karmic Law makes us all toe the mark. It makes all bend to its will. It makes all conform. It cannot be bought, influenced, altered or changed. It perceives no preference and grants no favors on the basis of political correctness, political party, wealth, power, position, prestige, gender, race, creed, nationality, educational status or religion. As aforementioned, Karma is *the* Supreme Law of this world and the sooner we reconcile ourselves to it the better.

Under Karmic Law, no one escapes his misdeeds or is denied receipt for his good deeds. Karmic Law is truly blind justice in action and rules this creation simply and matter of factly. Period.

As Saint Sawan Singh declares in *Spiritual Gems*: (Radha Soami Satsang Beas, Punjab, India, 3rd edition, 1965, Letter #103)

The law . . . operates without regard to persons.

Karma is the vehicle, not just of blind justice, but of absolute justice, and certainly not human justice, which is mercurial and precarious depending on who holds the cudgel of power. Karma is the irrepressible law of sowing and reaping, cause and effect, action and reaction, choice and consequence.

Karma is a very simple word; a simple law. It's a safe bet that most people know the phrase "sowing and reaping." The question is, "How many people believe it, believe that whatever we sow we reap?" Why do we know this? Because if people believed it, they wouldn't do many of the things they do or make the kinds of decisions they make. It's safe to say that most people create actions blindlessly and recklessly without so much as a nano thought of what they're doing or of the consequences of their actions or the repercussions of their choices.

Although people may have heard of the karma theory, many don't believe it because they see what appears to be a world full of injustice, as well as people committing crimes that ostensibly go unpunished. This leads people to exclaim, "Justice! What justice? The world is full of injustice. People sow evil deeds but never get penalized or punished for them." In other words, people feel such violators do not reap the deeds of their dark and nefarious sowing. Hence, the confusion.

Indeed, injustice may appear in the world, but in actuality there is no injustice at all in this world. There is perfect justice, even though we may not understand it. In reality, those who do evil deeds do eventually get their punishment, although not necessarily in *this* lifetime. As 20th Century Saint Sawan Singh states: (*With the Three Masters, Volume 1*, 5th Edition, Sewa Singh, Radha Soami Satsang Beas, p.181)

The wicked people, however, suffer heavy punishment for their sins in hell or in their future lives.

Therefore, just because evil doers appear to go unpunished in this life does not mean they escape penalties for their behaviors throughout their existence of many lives, in many forms. Everybody must pay for their bad deeds or receive proper compensation for their good deeds, just as Saint Sawan Singh states. It's simply a matter of when, where and how - all of which are in God's hands.

Seeds sewn must sprout. It's the law, whether we believe it or not; accept it or not; live by it or not. And, no, none of us is special, i.e., above the Law. We may think we're above the Law (especially human law) but we are uncompromisingly chained to Karmic Law, and sooner or later, in this life or the next, we will be forced, involuntarily, to submit to it - to its chains, shackles, whips and spankings or its soothing embrace of love, warmth, affection, approbation and applause.

If and when Karmic Law is functionally understood, it will not only change people's lives, it will revolutionize their existence. It would, therefore, behoove us all - collectively and individually - to think long and deeply on this Great Law we so lightly dismiss, disclaim and ignore because it's not dismissing, disclaiming or ignoring us. Bet on it.

Whether we subscribe to Karmic Law or not makes no difference. Our beliefs will not, cannot, negate it. Its reality was meticulously woven into the fabric of this creation from its inception. We will not be able to escape the consequences of our thoughts and deeds. They will rebound to us in a heap of reaping in spite of any weeping we will endure.

Richard Andrew King

Karmic Law never rests, never sleeps, never pauses, never stumbles, never takes a vacation. It is relentlessly operating with every breath we breathe, with every step we take, with every thought we think and with every act we perform – secretly or openly. We cannot hide from it, for it is invisible, just like gravity. If we are wise, we will apply it systematically to our thoughts and actions and not continue to ignore it because, without fail, it is not ignoring us.

KARMIC ATTRIBUTES

The opening sentence to this book reads:

Karma is the Supreme, Eternal, Universal, Immutable, Irrefutable, Inescapable, Inviolable, Irrevocable, Inexorable, Self-Operating Law of this Creation. The protracted definition is intentional in order to drive home the message of Karmic Reality and to keep the drum beat beating. Let's take a closer look at these ten attributes.

Supreme

Supreme signifies the highest in degree, rank, quality, authority, station. It is paramount, sovereign. Thus, karma is the highest Law, the determiner of justice in this world.

Eternal

*Eterna*l means everlasting, immortal, without end.

Universal

Universal references everyone, everywhere and every thing. Karma is omnipresent, pervasive, ubiquitous. There is no place where karma is not active.

Immutable

Immutable means that which cannot be changed or altered in any way. Thus, karma is fixed and is, indeed, a fixture of our existence in this world, just like air and water.

Irrefutable

Irrefutable indicates that which cannot be refuted, denied or proven to be false. Karma is incontrovertible and not open to be questioned. It exists by Divine Design, not by human construction.

Inescapable

Inescapable denotes the state of captivity, i.e., no escape. In many ways we are prisoners in this world because through past lifetimes we have woven a web of karmic fibers generated from a process of action and reaction. Verily, we live in a reticulated imprisoned environment of our own making.

Inviolable

Inviolable signifies that karma cannot be violated, harmed, trespassed or assaulted in any way. We can't defend ourselves from it. Rather, we need to work with it and utilize it to defend ourselves from ourselves and our actions. We do this by not doing things that endanger us or negatively impact our well-being or that of others unnecessarily.

Irrevocable

Irrevocable admonishes us that Karmic Law cannot be revoked, repealed or annulled. Karma is as integral to our lives as the sun.

Inexorable

Inexorable tells us karma is relentless, uncompromising, unforgiving and cannot be moved or stopped. Talk about a steam roller! We either get with the Karmic Program or get rolled over and crushed. Ignoring karma is disastrous to our lives.

Self-Operating

Self-Operating is, perhaps, the most critical aspect because it defines karma as functioning completely by itself. In other words, karma is an *automatic function* woven into the warp and woof, the fabric of this creation. It can't be stopped. It is working relentlessly every second of every minute of every hour of every day of every month, of every year, of every decade of every century of every millennium, ad infinitum. It will continue to operate until this creation is destroyed or dissolved, and only God knows when that will be.

THE KARMIC ALGORITHM

The Self-Operating function of karma brings us to the analogy of karma being an algorithm, which is a fitting metaphor for this computer age.

An algorithm is basically an unambiguous, designed, calculation process for solving problems or accomplishing an end. When this creation was designed by its Creator (universally identified as God), an algorithm was developed to govern the creation based on one simple idea:

What we do will be done to us.

Pretty simple, eh? *What we do will be done to us.* This is what is universally known as karma, and it is profound in spite of its simplicity. Karma is the governing algorithm and Law of this world. What we sow, we reap, and we cannot reap what we do not sow. Simple. Simple. Simple. It is not more complicated than that. Yet, this extremely simple idea remains ungrasped by the world at large. It's as if we're living in a blind stupor or in a cave or both, totally ignorant of the very Law that governs every move we make. Blindness could never be more blind.

KARMIC CIRCLES & CYCLES

Think for a moment of the life process. Everything revolves in circles. Seconds, minutes, hours, days, months, years, etc., all start at a single point in time, circle back to their starting point, and go around again.

Expanding this idea, we know the earth circles the sun and the sun circles the galaxy approximately every 230 million years (NASA). Most likely, the galaxy revolves around some centerpoint, too. So it is with all celestial bodies – they move in circular patterns, i.e., they rotate.

Next, think of numbers. They revolve in Cycles of Nine. The First 9 Cycle is from 1 through 9. The Second Nine Cycle starts at 10 (a 1 in reduction) and concludes at 18 (a 9 in reduction). The Third 9 Cycle is active from 19 (a 1 in reduction) through 27 (a 9 in reduction). And on and on it goes, forever.

And what else moves in circles and cycles? – our problems. Think about it. Each of us experiences certain problematic issues in our lives which keep circling and cycling back around, and around, and around again. This is associated with the cycle of numbers and can be known through numerology – the science of numeric coding defining and describing our lives, relationships and destinies.

This fact of life was noted by Pulitzer Prize winning American author, playwright and feminist of the early 20th Century, Edna St. Vincent Millay, who, although not a numerologist, sagaciously observed:

It's not true that life is one damn thing after another; it is one damn thing over and over.

If we assess our lives, we will see that St. Vincent Millay was absolutely correct in a general sense. Our problems, issues or situations in life revolve in circles and cycles just like every other aspect of this creation.

[Note: The science of numbers is fully treated and taught in *The King's Book of Numerology*tm series, currently containing twelve volumes as of 2019, available at RichardKing.net, Amazon.com and online retailers.]

Time, planetary bodies, numbers and personal issues all exist in a pattern of circles and cycles. Why would it be different with karma? In fact, it's not different. Karma circles and cycles, too. What we put onto the circle of life circles back to encircle us, eventually. Good or bad, positive or negative, hateful or loving, peaceful or turbulent – all will return to us one day. We cannot prevent this from happening. Such is Karmic Law.

FROM GOLDEN RULE TO GOLDEN LAW

We all know the Golden Rule: *Do unto others as you would have them do unto you.* This is a nice thought. However, it's just that, a nice thought but without teeth. However, when we apply Karmic Law to the Golden Rule, a Golden Law is generated which does have teeth. It reads:

Do unto others as you would have them do unto you
because as you do unto others so will it be done unto you!

With this addition, the Golden Rule becomes a Golden Law possessing an enormous bite. The "nice thought" morphs into an "executable mandate" of accountability which generates a reason to be nice and to avoid being naughty.

God doesn't prevent us from making choices, but He also doesn't prevent us from experiencing the consequences of those choices. In fact, the Karmic Algorithm mandates that we experience the same thing we create.

As the Bible states: (Galatians 6:7)

Be not deceived. God is not mocked, for whatsoever
a man soweth, that shall he also reap.

Saint Ravidas of the 15th/16th Century states: (*Guru Ravidas: Life and Teachings*, K. N. Upadhyaya, Radha Soami Satsang Beas, Punjab, India, 1982, p.46)

Whatever thou hast sewn, the same shalt thou reap.
No change in this shall there ever be.

The modern translation is:

Whatever you have sewn, the same shall you reap.
No change in this shall there ever be.

Ravidas also adds: (Ibid., p.183)

The fruit of action unfailingly overtakes the doer.

Buddha's statement mirrors that of Ravidas. He says:

If you fear pain, if you dislike pain, don't do an evil deed in open or secret. If you're doing or will do an evil deed, you won't escape pain. It will catch you even as you run away.

Seventeenth and Eighteenth Century Saint Dariya of Bihar corroborates this truth: (*Dariya Sahib - Saint of Bihar*, K.N. Upadhyaya, Radha Soami Satsang Beas, Punjab, India, 1987, p.357)

The sower of the poison cannot but be engulfed in the poison.

Sobering thoughts aren't they from the Bible, Buddha, Ravidas and Dariya of Bihar? What all of them are saying in their own way is that no one is smart enough, slick enough or powerful enough to neutralize the reactions to their actions. We are all doomed to experience what we create. What we sow will, not may, eventually catch up with us and force us to live whatever it was we placed onto the circle of life. In other words, we can run but we can't hide. Eventually, by Karmic Law, we all get caught.

Saint Charan Singh remarks in *Quest for Light*: (Radha Soami Satsang Beas, Punjab, India, 3rd edition, 1977, Letter #269)

The law of Karma, 'As you sow so shall you reap,' is working relentlessly and we are all reaping what we have sown in the past.

In *The Master Answers,* he states emphatically: (Radha Soami Satsang Beas, Punjab, India, 5th edition, 1980, Answer #609, p.490)

Nothing happens without karma.

He further declares: (Ibid., Answer #472)

Karma – nobody can escape, whether one believes it or not.

From the book *Dadu: The Compassionate Mystic* (K. N. Upadhyaya, Radha Soami Satsang Beas, Punjab, India, 2nd edition, 1980, p.177) comes this quote:

What thou hast not done will never befall thee;
only what thou hast done will befall thee.

Saint Sawan Singh in his classic work, *Spiritual Gems* (Radha Soami Satsang Beas, Punjab, India, 3rd edition, 1965, Letter #60), teaches:

As we sow, so shall we reap. Whatever we are reaping now, we, ourselves, have sown before. Therefore, we are the makers of our own fate.

And . . .

The Law of Karma is the principal law of the creation: as the action, so is the reward.

And . . .

The Karmic Law is inexorable and operates without regard to persons.

And . . .

The Karmic Law is supreme and inevitable and the sooner we reconcile ourselves with it the better.

In his book *The Science of the Soul*, Saint Jagat Singh states: (Maharaj Sardar Bahadur Jagat Singh, Radha Soami Satsang Beas, Punjab, India, 5th edition, 1977, p.98)

The Law of Karma is universal. It is the fixed and immutable law of nature. Each soul must reap what it has sown. Every soul shall have to bear the exact consequences of its actions.

He goes on to say: (Ibid., p.220)

The Law of Karma is a self-operating law of cause and effect. A seed sown must sprout. Whatever you sow now, you will have to reap either in this birth or the next. Every action produces reaction, which in turn produces further reactions and this vicious circle goes on forever.

And if specificity is still an issue, Saint Jagat Singh declares: (pp.195/196)

Not even a single grain that inadvertently enters your granary from a neighbor's field can go unaccounted. You simply must pay for what you get. The law is inviolable and it cannot be set aside. The payment may be either in kind, in coin, or by transfer of an equivalent good karma, but payment there must be.

This truth is echoed in the Bible: (St. Matthew 5:6)

> *Verily I say unto thee, Thou shalt by no means come out thence, till thou hast paid the uttermost farthing.*

Following is a brief sampling of how Karmic Law may generally manifest.

If we lie, we will be lied to.
If we kill, we will be killed.
If we love, we will be loved.
If we hate, we will be hated.
If we give, we will be given to.
If we abort, we will be aborted.
If we cheat, we will be cheated.
If we betray, we will be betrayed.
If we forgive, we will be forgiven.
If we steal, we will be stolen from.
If we nurture, we will be nurtured.
If we support, we will be supported.
If we help others, we will be helped.
If we obstruct, we will be obstructed.

If we vilify others, we will be vilified.

If we're kind, we will receive kindness.

If we adulterate, we will be adulterated.

If we deceive others, we will be deceived.

If we slander another, we will be slandered.

If we speak truth, truth will be spoken to us.

If we deny the truth, the truth will be denied to us.

In summation, mankind is governed by man's laws. However, the Creation is governed by God's laws, and the Supreme Law of this Creation is Karma – the Supreme, Eternal, Universal, Immutable, Irrefutable, Inescapable, Inviolable, Irrevocable, Inexorable, Self-Operating LAW of this Creation. Yet, it is amazing and tragic how the most universal and fundamental Law of this creation is so universally and fundamentally ignored.

We reap what we sow and we cannot reap what we do not sow. Whatever we do will be done to us. Karmic Law is a simple profound truth and no one escapes it – not you, nor I, nor any other living being in this world. Let those who hear, truly hear . . . and act accordingly.

It cannot be more simple. What we do will be done to us at some future time. By Karmic Law it is impossible for the reaping not to follow the sowing, for consequences not to follow cause, for reactions not to follow actions. Thus, there is perfect justice in the world, regardless of thought to the contrary.

Richard Andrew King

Therefore, it would be extremely prudent for us to think and reflect on our actions *before* we execute them. If we want a good life, a happy life, an harmonious life, especially moving forward, we must *live* by Karmic Law, not simply give lip service to it.

Because of karma's cyclical nature ad infinitum, we imprison ourselves by our own making. As Saint Charan Singh points out: (*Legacy of Love*, p.109)

A spider weaves its own net, then it finds itself a prisoner of that net.

Guru Nanak corroborates this paradigm: (*Guru Nanak: His Mystic Teachings,* J. R. Puri, Radha Soami Satsang Beas, Punjab, India, 2nd Edition, 1993, p.104)

In the web of its own actions is the whole world caught and it does not realize it.

When will we not just comprehend the reality of Karmic Law but actually live our lives based on its truth? Will we choose to remain blind and chained to it, or will we break free from its reticulated web of entrapment and rise higher into the Realm of Divine Consciousness?

JUSTICE

From *99 Poems of the Spirit*

Logic doesn't rule the world.
The Law of Karma does.
It is the way the world works
since the world was.
In counterpoint to justice lacking
in this world of women, men;
in Truth, there's total justice
from beginning to the end,
for Justice rules through Karma,
not through human laws.
Justice is Divinely based;
its roots in Godly Cause.
Think not there is no justice.
There is, but we're confined
to understand its workings
from this side of the Blind.
Remember, Karma is inexorable.
Its justice is unflawed.
There never is injustice
in the Hallowed Halls of God.

REAPING WEEPING

Forever have we planted seeds –
the fetters of our keeping;
and now we find ourselves distraught,
distressed, and reaping weeping.
We close our eyes and shun the Law,
unconcerned of havoc wreaking;
and now, with storms upon us,
we cry unceasing, reaping weeping.

So immersed in petty selves
and in life's treasures we were stealing,
we never paused to ponder
that one day we'd be reaping weeping.
It's hard to feel sympathy
for those who spend defeating
the very purpose of this life
as they scream, reaping weeping.

We do have choices in this life,
and if its Goodness we wish keeping,
then we should watch the seeds we're planting
or we'll be reaping weeping.

CHAPTER TWO

WHY KARMIC CONCERN?

"So," says John Doe, "I don't care about Karmic Law. I don't believe in it. Besides, we only live once, so what do I care about some philosophy expounding a past or future life, which I also don't believe in?"

Well, each to their own, but words to the wise: Saints understand the truth of karma and, arguably, their writings from age to age, culture to culture, language to language all confirm that Karmic Law is a reality of this creation.

Saints are highly evolved souls, to say the least. Their words, writings and teachings are profound and – another word to the wise – should not be ignored. This author has found their writings to be, spiritually, the highest, most complete and comprehensive on earth.

Saints do not come into this world to start a new religion. They come for one purpose and one purpose only – to enlighten souls of their connection to God and teach those souls the science of merging their soul with God, thus allowing them to escape from this netherworld. [For individuals interested in knowing more about Saints, the book *Messages from the Masters – Timeless Truths for Spiritual Seekers* is available at RichardKing.net/books, Amazon.com and online retailers].

And on another aside, beliefs are simply thoughts, not facts. They neither validate nor invalidate reality. Furthermore, many beliefs turn out to be false, though rigidly held at one time to be true by the entire world, such as the world being flat or being the center of the universe.

The teachings of Saints are not based on belief, conjecture or hearsay. They are based on *personal experience*, and this is what makes their teachings markedly convincing.

THE WHEEL OF TRANSMIGRATION

All Saints believe in the reality of Transmigration – the movement/migration of the soul via reincarnation (rebirth in a new body) through various living forms from vegetation to insect to ocean life to birds to animals to human. Transmigration is actually a condemnation of dying and being reborn over and over again in various bodily forms, not necessarily human, until or unless we can ascend into higher planes of existence and exit this lower dimension.

Transmigration is often associated with Indian religions such as Hinduism, Sikhism, Buddhism and Jainism. However, great thinkers such as Socrates, Plato and Pythagoras also believed in transmigration. As its truth is realized, Western cultures will follow suit as the deeper secrets of spirituality expand.

There is a belief that transmigration and reincarnation are New Age concepts. Actually, they're not. They're ages old. Pythagoras, for example, died approximately 495 years BCE (Before the Common Era). Socrates died in 399 BCE; Plato died approximately 417 BCE. These were three of the greatest thinkers in history and they lived well over 2,300 years ago. Verily, one could make the argument that Western understanding of spirituality is late to the party.

The process of transmigration is often referred to as the Wheel or Cycle of Transmigration, also known as The Wheel of Eighty-Four, Eighty-Four Lakhs, Chaurasi or simply "Wheel" for short. One lakh equals 100,000 units.

The Wheel of Transmigration is a construct of 8,400,000 forms of life into which the soul can incarnate. And here's the critical point: of this 8,400,000 forms of life, the highest form is man, and only man has the ability to know of God and merge his soul into the ocean of God's energy. This means that 8,399,999 other forms of life are left devoid of divine access. Only man has the privilege of being God-conscious. This is why the human body is sacred beyond belief and is referred to by Saints as the Top of Creation. Only in the human body can one know there's a God and even merge himself with God. How special it is to be human!

As the famous Indian Saint, Guru Nanak, states: (*Guru Nanak, His Mystic Teachings,* Professor J. R. Puri, Radha Soami Satsang Beas, 1982, 2nd Edition, p.283)

Precious is the human birth; only the saints know its worth.

And: (Ibid., p.341)

Men are victims of their evil passions and are dominated by their worldly attachments. They forget that the human birth is a very rare gift, the only one in eighty-four lakhs of species for attaining release from birth and death.

Nanak goes on to say: (Ibid., p.50)

Not only does God live within the human body, but it is only within this body that He manifests himself. Thus, it is doubly blessed.

From the Bible we read: (I Corinthians 3: 16)

Know ye not that ye are the temple of God and that the Spirit of God dwelleth in you? If any man defile the temple of God, him shall God destroy, for the temple of God is holy, which temple ye are.

If one is not convinced about the importance of the human body within the Wheel of Transmigration, the following quote from Saint Charan Singh should make one think deeply about the extreme and incredible gift each of us has been given. (*Quest for Light*, p.166)

The human body is not given to us in every birth. We get it only after millions of lives, and it is a very rare and precious gift not to be wasted upon the perishable things and objects of this world.

Millions of lives! We have been given this unbelievable gift of the human body – the Crown Jewel of all living forms in this creation – after eons of time enslaved in the Wheel of Transmigration in the other 8,399,999 forms of life! If this does not put things in perspective as to how utterly blessed we are as human beings, then what will?

How many of us take our temporal human body for granted, not knowing the immensity of goodness and opportunity it affords? And since human life is temporal, would it not be wise to make the most of its use while we can? Of course it would be, and we'd better, lest upon our death we are thrown back into the Wheel of

Eighty-Four, for God only knows how long. Contemplatingly, how many eons of time comprise 8,400,000 lives? We can't know, but let's hope we adopt the spiritual program of elevating our consciousness so we continue making upward progress on the Ladder of Life, thus avoiding the Wheel of Eighty Four and its unthinkable enslavement.

In consideration, Saint Jagat Singh offers the following warning which helps place this entire discussion of the Wheel of Transmigration in its proper perspective. (*The Science of the Soul*, p.38)

(Unfortunately), the true value of the human body is realized after death when man regrets that he has squandered his most precious possession. The result is that he has to go to hell or to lower births.

In his book, *The Dawn of Light*, Maharaj Sawan Singh comments: (Radha Soami Satsang Beas, Punjab, India, 1st edition, 1985, p.192)

In the cycle of transmigration, birth as a human being takes a long time to come again. Once the opportunity is lost, there is the cycle to go through. A slip from the top of a mountain means a heavy fall, and a stop on the way down is rare.

Guru Nanak weighs in: (*Philosophy of the Masters*, Vol. 1, Huzur Maharaj Sawan Singh, Radha Soami Satsang Beas, Punjab, India, p.30)

The cycle of transmigration is dreadful, and it is beyond the comprehension of the human intellect.

Swami Ji Maharaj, the Great Saint of Agra (19th Century), corroborates Saint Charan Singh's statement regarding transmigration: (*The Science of the Soul*, p.64)

This valuable body you got after roaming in millions of lower lives. Now do not lose it in vain pursuits. Take heed! Give your attention to Devotion. Have pity on your poor soul and save it from transmigration's wheel.

In capitalizing the word *Devotion* he is referencing the worship of God, adherence to Divine Laws, as well as the purification and perfection of our being.

Swami Ji Maharaj offers this dire and very sobering warning in his book *Sar Bachan: Book 2, Sayings*: (#86)

If, however, you don't believe in either what I say or in the writings of the Saints, the path of Transmigration lies before you. Walk upon it by all means.

THE KARMIC TRIAD

The triangle/triad is a representation of many life principles:

Activity/Passivity/Neutrality
Masculine/Feminine/Neuter
Positive/Negative/Balance

Father/Son/Holy Ghost

Master/Disciple/Word

Father/Mother/Child

Body/Mind/Spirit

In addition to these we can also add *The Karmic Triad* of Karma/Reincarnation/Transmigration.

The interrelationship between karma, reincarnation and transmigration is massively critical to our life in this incarnation because it allows us to make better, more health-engendering decisions; expand our understanding of life, not just of this incarnation but throughout our entire existence, and, therefore, plan for a better life or lives moving forward after this life ends.

By Karmic Law, what we do in this life, what we sow in this incarnation, becomes the seed of the harvest we will be forced to reap in the next life and/or lives. Once we know, we can never not know, so to begin living by Karmic Law now is not only great spiritual wisdom, it is the key to a better future beyond the grave, beyond this life.

There are those individuals who disclaim this process of transmigration by subscribing to the acronym Y.O.L.O. – You Only Live Once, which is not an uncommon delusion. Rather, it is a great deceit, a lie. Do not believe it.

Saint Sawan Singh states: (*Spiritual Gems*, p.116 & 81)

The principle of reincarnation is a fact. It is part of the Creator's scheme.

The law of transmigration . . . is far more real and inexorable than some people, in their shortsightedness, feel inclined to admit.

He also remarks: (*Philosophy of the Masters*, Vol. 1, p.27)

The law of transmigration is irrevocable.

And let's not forget Guru Nanak's warning, which gives more concerning validation of transmigration: (Ibid., p.30)

The cycle of transmigration is dreadful and it is beyond the comprehension of the human intellect.

Enough said at this point, which is that the process of transmigration is real and it would behoove us to follow the advice of these esteemed Saints.

So of what concern are the concepts of karma, reincarnation and transmigration to John Doe now? Would he dismiss the statements and advice of these Saints and Mystics so lightly?

It is our actions from moment to moment and day to day that determine if we are worthy of having a human body. If we sow actions that are not befitting of the extraordinary high rank of being human, of being the Top of Creation, then we may lose such a privilege and its potential and descend to lower forms of life for indeterminate periods of time. If this were the case, we would have to begin the upward journey all over again from some lower life form upward to human, hopefully to human, but of this there is no guarantee.

Therefore, the purer and more ethical our daily actions are will be to our benefit in the process of ascent on the Divine Ladder of Life. We should remember that what can go up can also go down and vice-versa. Where there is progress, there is also the potential of regress. But do we really want to risk falling from the esteemed pedestal we now inhabit? What a tragedy it would be for us to neglect the incredible opportunity of spiritual advancement while being in a human body and fall from such a great height.

Understanding transmigration, we need to take action now while we're guaranteed of the chance to advance. Once this life is passed and our human body is destroyed, we don't know what will happen, and we may not get the precious and priceless gift of a human form again for millions of lives and eons of time.

Frankly, it shouldn't even be a choice, for the choice is perfectly clear – keep moving Up. Make choices which are in keeping with spiritual life and law, never forgetting or dismissing Swami Ji's warning:

If, however, you don't believe in either what I say or in the writings of the Saints, the path of Transmigration lies before you. Walk upon it by all means.

KARMA

With every step we take let it be known –
we reap the fruit of all we've sown.
No innocent tear, no painful cry,
No sad misfortune strolling by.

We do the act, we plant the seed;
The Law exact, we reap the deed.
From life to life, from time to time,
Precise our sentence, cruel or kind.

No soul escapes, no soul defies,
We roam the Wheel for countless lives;
From birth to death, around we go
in Maze of Maya – tortured soul;
coming, going, endless forms,
blinded eye, countless storms.

Our only grand and saving grace –
to meet a Master face to face;
to beg His mercy for our life,
to end the turmoil and the strife;
to end the suffering, nightmare plight;
to bathe us in resplendent Light;
To free us from the hell we roam,
to guide, protect and take us Home.

KING OF LAWS

Whatever you are reaping now
you, yourself, have sewn before.
This is not lore, but Karma.

Whatever you have ever sewn
the same shall you reap and own.
This fact forever known as Karma.

Whatever you have never done
will never catch you as you run.
Good or bad you can't outrun your Karma.

Every action has reaction.
Every consequence its cause.
Karma is the King of Laws.

So, Dear Friend,

Be wise or foolish but take heed,
Every deed will make you bleed
or laugh or smile or cry.
Karma.

CHAPTER THREE

KARMIC HINDRANCES

Each of us is comprised of both good and bad karmas. If all our karmas were good, we'd be in some paradise; if they were all bad, we'd be in some hell. Thus, we possess both. Nobody is perfect in this world. We all have our faults, failings, sins, shortcomings, assets and liabilities.

This said, Saints describe five impediments to our spiritual progress which have been referred to by different Saints as hindrances, thieves, passions, poisons, perversions, enemies. Regardless of the name, they are detrimental to our well-being and Ascent. Like clinging vines they attach themselves to us, overwhelming us with their creeping, grasping, life-sucking tendrils, making it difficult for us to rid them from our being. Yet, we must rid ourselves of them if we're to move up the Ladder of Creation.

These five hindrances are: pride, anger, greed, attachment and lust. Every day we must battle these foes and ultimately rid ourselves of them if we're to succeed in climbing the Spiritual Ladder. Giving into them and allowing them to control us generates negative karma, adding more chains to our worldly enslavement.

PRIDE

We've all heard the Biblical saying: (Proverbs – 16:18)

Pride goeth before destruction,
and an haughty spirit before a fall.

How true is this maxim! I suspect most of us have allowed our pride to get in the way of our best intentions at some time or other, and history is replete with examples of individuals whose pride and contemptuous behavior have led to their fall – some falls mild, some falls medium and some falls of the Humpty-Dumpty variety where it's impossible to put the pieces back together again. The big falls are invariably the result of an ostentatious display of pomposity redlining in overdrive.

As we're all pretty aware, it's hard to tame our egos and keep them in check. Everybody's got one and with so many billions of people on the planet it's impossible to keep them from clashing at some time, and when the egos do clash, often for some silly or unjustifiable reason, just think how much bad karma they generate – negative energy placed onto the circle of life which will, assuredly and unfailingly, circle back to encircle the offender(s).

As an example, how many problems every second of every day around the world are generated by egos out of control at home, at work, on the road, in the supermarket, parking lot, playground, sports venue, neighborhood, restaurant, school, university or office? You name it. Anywhere and everywhere on a moment-to-moment basis around the world pride raises its ugly head and creates problems, mostly unwarranted but all problematic.

And the cause of such prideful experiences? A litany of causes could be generated but a few would be jealousy, envy, hatred, bitterness, resentment, selfishness, personal insecurity, sanctimony, narcissism, egocentricity, power trips. And for what? Bad feelings on both sides? Creating an environment that's difficult to live or work in? Generating discord and ill will?

So what is the antidote for our excessive pride, our egos out of control? The answer is simple, *humility* – one of the greatest of virtues, but one of the most difficult to express.

In fact, one of the definitions of humility is "freedom from pride, from an oversaturated ego." But to get rid of our ego, we have to put our self-importance on the back burner, maybe eat a little crow or at least keep our mouth shut. That can be challenging. Hence, the saying from *The Black Belt Book of Life – Secrets of a Martial Arts Master*: (RichardKing.net/books, Amazon.com; online retailers)

Arrogance is the highest form of weakness;
Humility is the highest form of strength.

This is an interesting but true statement. Too often there are those individuals who believe that arrogance is a sign of strength and humility a sign of weakness. The reality is just the reverse. Arrogance requires no self-control or discipline but humility requires great discipline and self-control. Humility is the stronger by far; arrogance the weaker, for sure.

In fact, is it not true that the greatest and strongest souls in history were marked by a high level of humility? Anyone can be arrogant. We witness that every day, but humility is a virtue which is, sadly, seldom on display in the world. Why? Because humility is difficult to master and manifest. It requires self-abnegation, discipline and self-control – all challenges for the self-centered ego.

ANGER

What human has never been angry? It's a natural emotion but one that, nonetheless, is highly destructive and injurious to both the recipient and the perpetrator if not kept under control. Hence, the need for discipline.

One nuclear blast of anger, just one, can destroy an entire life of goodness and damage our relationships, making them difficult to mend and heal.

Following are some valuable quotes regarding anger.

Saint Kabir: (*Kabir The Great Mystic*, Isaac A. Ezekiel, Radha Soami Satsang Beas, Punjab, India, 4th edition, 1979, p.400)

Anger is a great enemy of the spiritual path; a single spark can cause a million sins, and all devotion and good deeds are wasted by a single wave of anger caused by ego.

Saint Charan Singh: (*Quest for Light*, Letter #337)

Anger is a sign of weakness and lack of clear thinking. If you were to know what great damage one rush of anger does to your liver, you would never get angry.

Damage to one's liver with one rush of anger? How much is anger damaging our other internal organs? Frightening.

Pythagoras:

In anger we should refrain both from speech and action.

Saint Sawan Singh: (*The Dawn of Light*, p.81)

Anger should give way to calmness, avarice to contentment.

Keep your mind broad, for the mind that harbors anger has lost its peace. (Ibid., p.188)

A heart filled with love cannot contain anger. (*Spiritual Gems*, Letter #20)

Keep your thoughts pure. It is lust and anger that make the mind impure and prevent spiritual development. (Ibid., Letter #64)

From Saint Jagat Singh: (*The Science of the Soul*, p.69)

Anger burns up all that is noble.

Lust degrades and disgraces; anger consumes and destroys; greed hardens and petrifies; attachment seduces and procrastinates and egotism distorts and deceives. (Ibid., p.70)

The five passions – lust, anger, avarice, attachment and pride are commissioned by the Negative Power to mislead both mind and soul and make trouble for them. (Ibid., p.104)

From Swami Ji Maharaj: (*Sar Bachan*, Entry #16)

Anger is the instrument of Kal (the Negative Power/Satan). *Do not let it enter into you.*

Bible: Psalms 37:8:

Refrain from anger, and forsake wrath! Fret not yourself; it tends only to evil.

Bible: Proverbs 15:18

A hot-tempered man stirs up strife, but he who is slow to anger quiets contention.

Bible: Ecclesiastes 7:9

Be not quick in your spirit to become angry, for anger lodges in the bosom of fools.

Bible: James 1:19, 20

Know this, my beloved brothers: let every person be quick to hear, slow to speak, slow to anger; for the anger of man does not produce the righteousness of God.

Obviously, from all the quotes above, anger is a universal trait that certainly needs addressing. So what is the antidote for anger? The answer is *forgiveness* and *forbearance.*

Forgiveness means to let go of one's resentment toward another individual. Forbearance means to control oneself and be patient when provoked. In other words, let us not instantly explode at someone, some thing or some event but curb our knee-jerk reaction of anger. By doing this we keep from inflaming the situation and avoid generating negative karma. A little self-reflection of the times we have exploded in a fit of anger and the resulting negative impact on another or others will help us learn to exercise some self-control, forgiveness and forbearance.

GREED

Greed is defined as an excessive, even ravenous, desire for something. Usually greed is associated with money and material things, but there is greed for power, status, fame, fortune, celebrity, popularity, etc.

When greed becomes compulsive and blind, it becomes hazardous to one's well-being, as well as that of others. Just stop and think of all the tension, anxiety, turmoil and hatred generated by an individual who takes, and takes, and keeps on taking to the detriment, discomfort and hardship of others.

As Mahatma Gandhi observed:

There is a sufficiency in the world for
man's need but not for man's greed.

In other words, there's never enough for a greedy man. His thirst for money, power, fame and status is unquenchable.

The following quote, attributed to Buddha, has several versions, the most concise being:

Give a man a mountain of gold and he'll want two.

Let's be clear, money in itself is not evil. Money has done wondrous things in this world because the world runs on money and commerce. It is the love, obsession and hording of money to the detriment of others that is evil.

As Saint Charan Singh says: (*Quest for Light*, Letter #101)

Please remember that money and wealth in itself is not evil. It is only its wrong use and improper application that is objectionable.

Money is meant for the good of everyone, but when, because of excessive, rapacious greed, people are negatively impacted, then money gets a bad reputation with negative karma of the miser being guaranteed.

Often greed is a manifestation of a poverty-stricken consciousness. For example, an individual who makes $60,000 an hour but deprives her gardener of a requested raise from $10/hour to $15/hour, is definitely manifesting a poverty-stricken consciousness.

It seems unbelievable, doesn't it, this sad but unfortunately true incident of a gardener being denied a mere $5/hour raise when his employer was making a massive sum of $60,000/hour! One can only guess at the future negative karma of such a heartless and greedy soul.

Perhaps, however, in another life the circumstances were reversed. Maybe the gardener was the wealthy one who denied a servant (now his employer) a requested raise and his greedy karma is now catching up with him. We can't know for sure but, this said, it is always wise to act on the principles of generosity and graciousness rather than being pennywise and karma foolish, if not karma ignorant and karma bound. Furthermore, it's better to be God rich and money poor than money rich and God poor. Publilius Syrus was a Latin writer from the 1st Century BCE. He makes this sentient and succinct observation: (*Moral Sayings*)

God looks at the clean hands, not the full ones.

This begs the question, "How clean are our hands?"

From a destiny perspective, however, Saint Charan Singh asserts: (*Quest for Light*, Letter #242)

One cannot and does not get a whit more nor
a penny less than what is in his destiny.

And the sober truth is: (Ibid., Letter #107)

Every single penny that we receive from anybody shall have to be repaid somehow in this life or in a future one. Everything in this whole universe has its price, so eventually one always has to pay for what one receives.

On another note, it may be of some use for us to understand that chains of gold are still chains. People may live in golden towers on a golden mountain on a golden world but until the karma of their existence in this world is reconciled and negated, they will still be slaves in this creation. True freedom will only be realized when our soul escapes from this Netherland of duality, of positive and negative karma, and returns Home to its true abode of Oneness, Love and Light.

The antidote for greed is *contentment*, being satisfied with who we are, where we are, what our destiny holds for us and, more importantly, what God gives to us. By remaining content, we remain balanced and centered and therefore more able to live a joyful life. The following anonymous quote is quite germane to the subject of greed.

The richest man in the world is not the one who has the most, but the one who needs the least.

When we crave for nothing, how rich are we? When we are consumed with always wanting more and more and more, how impoverished are we? How anxiety-saturated are we? How miserable are we? How poor are we, really?

ATTACHMENT

The challenging aspect of attachment is that it binds us, often blindly, to ideas, things, people, organizations, philosophies, etc., that immobilize us, preventing us from making beneficial changes that would liberate us from concepts, ideas and beliefs which do not serve our highest and best good but rather enslave us to this world.

Political parties are an excellent example of such attachment. How often do we see political groups voting en masse without even weighing both sides of an issue to arrive at a workable balance?

It's very common, for instance, for new members coming into a political party to be told to toe the mark, mind their place, and not to dissent from what the party line holds. Where is the chance to think for one's self in such a situation? Such people are forced, by attachment, to become nothing more than lemmings following the Pied Piper of their party.

Such attachment destroys the potential of new ideas, which could be beneficial. In such situations, freedom of thought is not only discouraged but stifled, shut down and crushed under the hammer of attachment. The message is, "If you want to get along, you must go along." Is this a great formula for stimulation, positive change and the advancement of society – conforming to an enshackled state of thought, beset with the disease of lemmingitis?

Such attachment not only makes us blind, it makes us foolish and stupid. When we're whole, we think and act on our own conscience and never capitulate to someone else's thoughts and demands simply based on our attachment to them. True thinkers, true leaders, stand alone and make their own decisions. They are brave and rare, indeed. Followers go along to get along and ultimately forfeit their individual sovereignty in the process. Such a shame.

Families, unfortunately, can also be a deterrent to one's place, peace or acceptance in the family unit because of attachment. For example, maybe the traditional religion of a family puts pressure on one or more family members to adhere to what is custom rather than what they or others in the family may choose as their religion. Such attachments can be extraordinary impediments to family harmony, often generating states of disharmony, or worse.

However, one's first obligation in life is to God, always. Families are secondary to one's spiritual connection. All individuals in the family should be able to make their own decision as to the religion or spiritual path they choose to follow, not what the family demands they follow.

Individual sovereignty trumps familial tradition or demand. The truth of life is that after this life ends we will go where our attachments are. If our attachment is to God, we will go with Him. If our attachments are to a family, we will gravitate to it.

This said, let's be clear. Families are critical to a well-functioning society and culture, but they are worldly by definition, design and karma. Our relationship with God is sacrosanct, primary, primal. Always and forever, our absolute focus in this life should be on God first, on the Creator of us and our relationship with Him or that Power. To do otherwise would be an inversion of Reality.

People are free souls. Their autonomy is sanctified. For a family to deny or discourage another family member from following his/her own heart is wrong. Karmically, when we deny others their freedom, our freedom will be denied to us. We sow, we reap. That's the Law, and if we demand attachment without respecting another's right to choose for themselves the path they want to follow, then the same demands we forced on others will eventually, in this life or a future life, come full circle and be forced upon us. It's inescapable. When we deny freedom to others, freedom will be denied to us. Simple. Exact. True. Profound.

Attachment is also on full display in the world of athletics, which do have their positive side but whose negative side can be challenging because over-enthusiastic fans of a team can create problems, even lethal problems, as have historically happened in some sports.

Athletics are an excellent way to develop one's character and skill, as well as offering an outlet for fun, positive emotion and competition. However, being heavily attached to a team can cause problems, fights, disturbances and states of imbalance, and this latter aspect is problematic. Once we're out of balance, problems ensue. Furthermore, if we rigidly cling to a team and are emotionally and psychologically so entangled with it that we develop physical, even mental, problems, that is not good, obviously, and demands introspection and healthful adjustment.
One metaphor for the pejorative aspects of attachment is of a barnacle stuck to a rock by or in the ocean. It's hard for the barnacle to free itself, and so it is trapped in a state of "stuckness." As long as it is attached and stuck, it will never be free.

We humans can be like barnacles stuck to a rock. In such a case, how can we be free? Answer: we can't. Our attachment to the rock prohibits our freedom. Similarly, our attachment to worldly ways, material things, people, old worn out beliefs, organizations, delusions, etc., negate our freedom and spiritual ascent because they keep us stuck to a rock. We must be free to move on, to move up. We cannot be free when we're stuck to a rock regardless of the rock's composition. Such attachment becomes a huge negative in our life, not a positive. This is a rock solid fact.

Introspectively, we would be well-served to think about our personal attachments and how they limit us, even deny us our freedom. Now, to be sure, a compromise between security and freedom can be reached but it must be within the domain of practicality and common sense.

The antidote for attachment is *discrimination* - the process or action of making a distinction as to the type and degree of attachment. If we're fully attached to God, we will automatically detach from the world. However, if we're fully attached to the world, we can't be attached to God, at least not fully. It's either one or the other. Sitting astride a fence gets us nowhere but stultified in a state of indecision and malaise, not to mention great discomfort.

Since the purpose of having a human body is to become God Realized, it makes common sense that we attach ourselves to a spiritual, divine way of life. We can certainly choose to attach ourselves to the world, but such attachment is, literally, a dead end. How can a balloon go up when it is tethered to the ground by anchors and chains? Obviously, it can't. Hence, our attachment needs to be to God, to the divinity of life, if we choose eternal life in Heaven and beyond or eternal life in hell and below. It's our choice but, as we know, every choice has its consequences. We sow, we reap, and we cannot reap what we do not sow. If we continually live by spiritual principles, we will eventually sever the chains which bind us to this material/carnal world. If we cling to worldly rocks we'll end up chained, enshackled and enslaved by the world. Either way, our attachments rule.

LUST

The fifth and final member of the Karmic Hindrances is *lust*, and by all spiritual accounts it is the absolute worst and most powerful of the group. The karma derived from lust is highly deleterious to spiritual development, as the following quotations reveal.

Saint Sawan Singh: (*Spiritual Gems*, Letter #24)

Lust is passion or indulgence in the sensual desires as opposed to self-control, but in its wide sense it means all outward tendencies of the mind.

He further comments: (Ibid., Letter #162)

Keep your thoughts pure. It is lust and anger that make the mind impure and prevent spiritual development.

Says Saint Charan Singh: (*Quest for Light*, Letter #174)

Lust in itself is the deadliest of sins.

And: (Ibid., Letter #38)

Lust . . . cuts at the very root of spirituality and devotion.

And: (*Divine Light*, Radha Soami Satsang Beas, 4th Edition, 1976, p.300)

Lust and love of God are poles apart and cannot remain together in a man's heart. When one comes, the other goes.

And: (Ibid., p.279)

The soul and the mind tend downward with lust and expand with anger.

And: *(Quest for Light*, Letter #237*)*

Regarding lust, please remember that this is the most potent weapon in the armory of the Negative Power to pull down a soul to the lowest level.

Saint Jagat Singh declares: (*The Science of the Soul*, p.79)

Beware! No action in this world goes without bearing fruit. Every action has its reaction. The worst reaction is that of lust.

Guru Ravidas warns: (*Guru Ravidas*, p.176)

The affliction of lust is the foremost trap of the world. None so entrapped has ever attained the Truth.

From the Bible, Galatians 5:16-17:

Walk in the Spirit and ye shall not fulfill the lust of the flesh.

The antidote for lust is *chastity*, generally defined as restraining from sexual intercourse. This can be difficult, especially in a culture where chastity is commonly ridiculed while promiscuity is celebrated. However, on the spiritual path chastity is celebrated and promiscuity reproved as a moral standard. The worldly path is diametrically opposed to the spiritual path. Hence, the drastic difference in sexual ideologies.

The opposition of sexuality between a worldly life and spiritual life is clear when we consider that sexual energies are primarily housed in the body's lowest energy centers while spiritual energies are located in the head. This is why paintings of Saints are depicted with auras around their heads, not their genitalia.

Too, how can we go North when we're going South? How can we detach from the carnal world when we're constantly attaching ourselves to it? Sexual energies retard, if not negate, the potential of spiritual ascent. Sexual energies and spiritual energies reside at opposite ends of the body spectrum. Hence, a tug-o-war and its natural opposition. This explains Saint Charan Singh's quote that *lust and love of God are poles apart.*

Saints are well aware of the power of the sexual instinct and, therefore, recommend a married life where sexual energies can be managed efficiently without jeopardizing one's spiritual progress. However, Saints do not endorse a promiscuous lifestyle of "free love" because it only adds more karma to one's already heavily-laden karmic burden.

What must be remembered is that the Saint's task is to enlighten souls and assist them in climbing the Spiritual Ladder and merging their individual souls with God. Saints are not concerned with worldly matters, only spiritual matters and liberating the soul from this world.

Sexuality is based in worldly, material, carnal expression. How can one be ultimately free of the world when drenched in material energies? Answer: it can't be. This is why Saints suggest a self-controlled and restricted sexual life. The more sexual encounters, the more karma, the more burden. Therefore, the impossible ability to advance up the Spiritual Ladder is the result, in part, of a promiscuous lifestyle. This is more fully described in the next chapter, *Karma of Free Love*.

In summation, the quality of our life is determined by the purity of our actions. These Five Hindrances – Pride, Anger, Greed, Attachment and Lust – are not only the enemies each of us has to fight every day if our goals are to be successful in our spiritual pursuits, but they also generate massive amounts of karma which, in turn, shackle us to this nether world.

We can't avoid these Five Poisons. They are fixtures of this creation. We have no choice but to engage and defeat them in the battle for our Ascent. If our goals are not in keeping with a spiritual life but rather a worldly life, then that's a personal choice we have to make. But what's the option? Spiritually speaking, there is no option except to keep doing our level best to fight and win. As the Bible states in St. Matthew 10:22: *He that endureth to the end shall be saved.*

KARMIC SEEDS

© Richard Andrew King

Killing seeds; destructive seeds
of ego, anger, lust, attachment, greed
planted, fed and watered
yield demon deeds.
Violence fills the tube,
video games the screen;
poison seeds, once planted
make the world mean.
Karma is a simple Law
but blinded we've become;
In quest of special interest,
desires make us dumb.
We give not a second thought,
to actions that we own;
oblivious to Karmic Law,
we reap what we have sewn,
and our actions make us captive,
through reactions we must serve;
but when the pain's upon us,
we rant and rave—what nerve!

We act so stunned and outraged,
indignant. "Who's to blame?"
"Certainly, not us," we cry!
Yet, deeds from seeds remain

the inviolable possession
of the doer of the deed,
and there is no escaping
the Law which supersedes
all our wants and wishes
in spite of what we plead.
In Netherland the Law demands,
we eat the fruit of all our seeds.
Hence, we should be forever wise,
'cause sure as fires burn,
the promise of God's Karmic Law
is that our seeds, as deeds, return!

CHAPTER FOUR

KARMA OF FREE LOVE

The karma of those who practice "Free Love" (promiscuous sexuality) is antithetical to one's spiritual progress because it increasingly adds more weight to one's already over-burdened storehouse of karma via the entanglement of souls, as discussed previously. As this chapter explains, "free love" is not free at all but rather quite enslaving, even condemnatory.

THE ENERGY OF CONNECTION

The first thing to realize is that each of us is an energetic being operating within a human body, or more exactly, a human suit. Think of an astronaut. He wears a space suit to protect him from potential dangers, but he is not the suit. The astronaut is a living being housed in a space suit. Likewise, we humans are living energetic beings housed in a human body, a human suit, but we are not our body. This is key. We are energy.

Sexually, when our energies mix with others during sexual intercourse while in a human body we overlook the fact that it is our *energies* that are primarily intermixing. Our bodies are simply the worldly mechanisms facilitating the connection, just as the words on this page are facilitating a message generated by living energy via the mechanism of fingers typing on a material keyboard.

And here's the critical point: while bodies can be separated relatively easily after sexual intercourse, the mixing energies cannot be separated, if at all. This creates massive problems spiritually because our spirits are energy, and the spiritual path focuses on the purification of that energy while the worldly path focuses on the carnal pleasures of the material body.

Think on this metaphor. Take a gallon can of yellow paint, a gallon can of blue paint and mix them thoroughly in a two gallon can. From this admixture, we get two gallons of green paint, right? Now here's the problem: separate the green paint back into its yellow and blue forms. It can't be done. The mixture is permanent.

Likewise, when we mix our energies with those of another person via sexual intercourse, we are generating a third energy which cannot be easily separated. When this process is continually repeated through multiple sexual encounters and partners, massive amounts of karma generate a web of seemingly inextricable energetic entrapment, bondage and imprisonment.

Such karmic loads greatly interfere with our ability to climb the Spiritual Ladder. In fact, they keep us from doing just that, forcing us to become increasingly shackled to this material dimension even more than before we engaged in yet another sexual encounter. In leading such an existence of so called "free love," we have done nothing but add to the fetters of our material and bodily enslavement. Truthfully, indulging in "free love" is not free at all. It is just the opposite, creating karmic chains binding us to this world.

For example, bodies can detach easily, as mentioned, but what about our minds and spirits? Their energy can't detach because the mind houses memories, images, feelings, conversations and a myriad of experiences with every lover we take or have taken. How can all these mental, emotional and psychological entanglements be undone? How can we be free with all the baggage we accumulate from the amalgam of our "free love" interactions? Can we press a magic button in our head that automatically makes us forget about our sexual involvements with others and everything attached to them? No. See the problem? Every sexual lover we have generates its own web of entrapment from which it is practically impossible to escape. To paraphrase Buddha:

Fifty loves, fifty woes. No loves, no woes.

THE DISEASE FACTOR

Furthermore, what about the potential of contracting some sexually transmitted disease or infection which increases the complexity of the karma. The CDC (Centers for Disease Control and Prevention) states, *There are dozens of STDs* and that *20 million new infections occur every year in the United States* (https://www.cdc.gov/std/). STD, of course, stands for sexually transmitted disease. STI stands for sexually transmitted infection. Twenty million new infections every year in the United States alone? What about the rest of the world?

How does any sexually transmitted disease not have a negative impact on someone, let alone millions of people? How much angst, concern, pain, suffering, turmoil, discomfort, sorrow and remorse, etc., are generated by STDs and STIs which, of course, are generally contracted through some form of sexual interaction?

How is having an STD/STI not enslaving? How can one feel free, light-hearted, cheerful, joyful and positive when beset with such diseases? Answer: no one. There is no freedom when struck with any disease. Rather, there is struggle, the degree of which is determined by the severity of the disease. To be sure, "free love" does have its shackles and chains in more ways than one.

The only sure way to be free of the negative effects of today's "free love," promiscuous, permissive lifestyle is to abstain and not engage in sexual intercourse at all. Notwithstanding the pain, angst, turmoil and disease caused by STDs/STIs in both body and mind, what about the immense karmic burden generated in the process? To this point, Guru Nanak remarks: (*Guru Nanak*, p.284)

If thou treadest the path of virtue,
sorrow will not dog thy footsteps.

Guru Ravidas makes a germane point regarding our struggle in these matters of sexuality: (*Guru Ravidas*, p.78)

Powerful are our senses and weak is our discrimination,
and spirituality entereth not our understanding.

In the same work Ravidas states: (Ibid., p.176)

The affliction of lust is the foremost trap of the world. None so entrapped has ever attained the Truth. Why shouldst thou be delighted and comforted in it?

Saint Charan Singh notes: (*Quest for Light*, Letter #492)

Sex is a natural instinct and a powerful one, too. Therefore, the Saints prefer a householder's life where the chances of one going astray from the path of morality are minimized. To stray away from the path of morality results in a very heavy burden, so a controlled householder's life is always preferable. (Note: by "householder's life" is meant a married life)

As a preventive strategy of avoiding the negative aspects of any behavior, Saint Dadu simply says: (*Dadu*, p.18)

Hold pure, stay pure and say pure.
Take the pure, give the pure.

Dadu's advice is simple, direct, effective and truthful. If we always do that which is pure, we will avoid the deleterious effects of impure choices and the heavy karmic burdens associated with them, both in the present and future.

THE DILUTION/POLLUTION FACTOR

Another issue. Even if a person does not contract one of the many debilitating STDs or STIs, there is another potential negative effect confronting those who choose a polyamorous lifestyle – the dilution and pollution of one's own innate energy.

Too, if there were no physical, emotional, psychological, financial or familial problems associated with many loves and lovers, there still remains the karma generated between all parties, karma which will have to be neutralized before we can return Home. Reconciling such Karmic Bonds could take innumerable lives. The fact remains that the more lovers we take, the more vast and intricate our Karmic Web becomes. There's no escaping this reality.

Another important concern involving the Karma of Free Love, is that of our purity, wholeness, health and well-being as an individual. When our personal energies mix with those of another individual, they (our energies) become not only diluted but also polluted with the lover's energies, not to mention any physical diseases or infections plaguing the other party which we may contract in the sex act. This Dilution/Pollution Factor generates a double dose of negative karma.

Such a quid-pro-quo of sex and its temporal pleasure in exchange for what we may lose in ourselves, and/or acquire in terms of disease and other problems, is a dangerous and foolish bargain. Is the experience of sexual carnal sensation in a brief encounter really worth the potential cost? Should not the long term risk outweigh the short-lived pleasure? Where is the wisdom of such a choice?

By diluting and adulterating our own energy, we destroy the purity of who we were at birth. With such a continual process of sexual Dilution/Pollution, we ultimately lose sight and feeling of our intrinsic self and its worth. Eventually, we may not even know ourselves because we have so diluted the inherent, pure, natural energy we were born with.

Where, for example, are the joy-filled, happy, positive, smiling faces in today's society? People are in such a rush, impatient, short-tempered, hostile, angry, even hateful. Is this not, in part, a symptom of today's promiscuous society and the Dilution/Pollution Factor?

Too, this is definitely an age where trust among people in relationship is waning rapidly, is it not? It seems that sleeping with whomever one wishes, whether one is in a relationship or not, overpowers choices of honesty, fidelity, devotion, discipline, self-control, temperance. The lust of passion is dominating a landscape where virtue is almost non-existent. Yet, personal character is of the utmost importance when considering the spiritual life.

Saint Sawan Singh states: (Spiritual Gems, Letter #117)

Purity of character is the fundamental basis on which the edifice of spiritual progress is to be built.

And: (Ibid., Letter #176)

Character is the foundation upon which rises the spiritual edifice. As long as one is a slave of the senses, talk of spirituality is a mockery. . . The first essential step to a spiritual life is character. One may deceive one's friends, relatives, and even oneself but the Power within is not deceived.

Saint Jagat Singh remarks: (*The Science of the Soul*, p.20)

High moral character is most essential for spiritual progress.

Saint Charan Singh comments: (*Divine Light*, p.181)

Sex is a natural instinct and to some extent its satisfaction is necessary. But its only purpose, as intended by God, is the procreation and propagation of the species. It should not be made a means of dissolute indulgence and pleasure, as that causes great degradation of the mind, soul and character. A disciplined life is always best.

And: (Ibid., p.300)

A high moral character is a condition precedent to God-Realization. Lust and love of God are poles apart and cannot remain together in a man's heart. When one comes, the other goes.

And: (*Quest for Light*, Letter #221)

The first prerequisite of a gentleman or a lady is a good moral character. If that is not there, what else is left?

The great Helen Keller remarks:

Character cannot be developed in ease and quiet. Only through experience of trial and suffering can the soul be strengthened, ambition inspired, and success achieved.

Famous American political figure and First Lady of the United States, Eleanor Roosevelt, affirms:

Only a man's character is the real criterion of worth.

Where in today's world is character placed on the pedestal requisite to its value? It may be a fair question to ask if the majority of people even place character on a pedestal or in a high position relative to their needs. We may talk about character, but do we honestly practice it and place it in its rightful position of life's priorities, i.e., at the top? Talk is cheap; walking our talk is difficult but obligatory if our goal is Divine Ascent.

Truly, character is critical to our well-being and an antidote to the Dilution/Pollution dilemma. And what is the foundation of character? Answer: virtue in all its forms including discipline, trust, devotion and fidelity.

SEXUAL CONSIDERATIONS

Kabir was a great Saint of the 15th/16th Centuries. He gives great attention to the subject of promiscuous sexuality in his writings because of its dangers. From *Kabir The Great Mystic* by Isaac A. Ezekiel (Radha Soami Satsang Beas, 4th edition, 1979, p.274) we read:

Promiscuous sex indulgence stands on a different footing. Just as Kabir condemned it, it has been condemned by all Saints and all scriptures.

This statement runs contrary to the worldly mindset of the "Free Love" culture. But then again, Saints are not concerned about worldly ways but spiritual ways, and as has been mentioned, the worldly lifestyle and spiritual lifestyle are diametrically opposed, comprised of opposite ideas moving in opposite directions with opposite goals.

Kabir asserts: (Ibid., p.277)

Sex indulgence is the lowest of human activities. That men should be at all proud of it surpasses understanding.

Few Saints are as brutally direct as Kabir. He tells it like it is because he understands what is at risk - one's very soul. The following quotes are a sampling from *Kabir The Great Mystic* (pp.396-397). They focus on the "strange woman," in other words, a promiscuous woman. But the same can also be said of the "strange man," a promiscuous man. Therefore, in the context of the following quotes, "woman" is a reference to lascivious behavior by either man or woman. It must be remembered that Kabir was speaking to a culture of the 15th/16th Centuries - a different time. This said, the principles and spiritual consequences of promiscuous sexuality, i.e., "Free Love," for both sexes remain as true today as they were then and will always remain true. Times may change; language may change, but truth never changes.

A few of Kabir's thoughts are these:

A strange woman brightens her eyes with collyrium and charms men by the way she does her hair. On her hands she puts sweet-smelling Mehndi and looks alluring; but truly in reality, she is a veritable tiger, devouring thee to pieces.

The company of a strange woman leads us straight to hell fire, from which a million efforts cannot save thee; thou wilt most surely be a captive and a plaything of the Angel of Death who knoweth all thy deeds.

A strange woman is much like a very sharp bright sword, and few are they who escape her most alluring charms; enter not into intimacy with her, even if she be made of gold.

A strange woman's love is really just like filth, containing not a particle of goodness in it. Like the ocean's fish, nothing can rid her of the evil smell however much she may be washed and washed again.

A strange woman leads thee straight to hell. Remember, she is bright and burning fire; if thy hands touch her, they will be severely burnt.

And finally . . .

A cobra has two hoods, but a woman possesses twenty; and she uses all of them to sting thee to thy death.

Of course, there will be those individuals who scorn, mock and rail against Kabir's words, especially in this age where promiscuity, not virtue, is promoted, promulgated and celebrated. Regarding this plight, Kabir states: (Ibid., p.402)

The wicked look on virtue with contempt, for sinning is to them so great a pleasure. The house-fly wings its way to feed on filth, and flies away from fragrance.

From Guru Nanak we read: (*Guru Nanak: His Mystic Teachings*, p.377)

Men's hearts are filled with lust and they run after women. They lose their poise and their sense of honor.

And this Nanak quote, aforementioned: (Ibid., p.164)

If thou treadest the path of virtue, sorrow will not dog thy footsteps.

Or in contemporary language:

If you tread the path of virtue, sorrow will not dog your footsteps.

From *St. John – The Great Mystic* by Saint Charan Singh (Radha Soami Satsang Beas, 4th edition, 1978, p.23) comes this statement:

Those who love evil and bad deeds and are victims of the senses always want to live in darkness and want to remain immersed in sensual pleasures. But those who do good deeds want to live in the light.

And isn't this the whole crux of this discussion, of this book – that *those who do good deeds want to live in the light*? But "living in the light" is a spiritual science, not a mere worldly philosophy. It takes work, sacrifice, dedication and determination to do so, but few people will choose to live in the light because the world's material/carnal energies are quite magnetic and seductive.

As Saint Ravidas says quite honestly: (*Guru Ravidas: Life and Teachings*, pp. 78 and 153 respectively)

The path to God is steep and difficult.

And so there is no mistake . . .

Devotion is not an amusement.

In plain words, spirituality is not a game or mere conversation topic. It is work; it requires devotion and dedication. Yet, the rewards are there, eventually.

The Bible is also very clear on the subject of promiscuous sexual behavior, i.e., fornication. From 1 Corinthians 6: 13, we read:

Now the body is not for fornication, but for
the Lord; and the Lord for the body.

And from St. Matthew 15: 19 & 20 . . .

For out of the heart proceed evil thoughts, murders, adulteries, fornications, thefts, false witness, blasphemies: These are the things which defile a man.

How can we live in the light and ascend the Divine Ladder of spirituality if we are defiled, i.e., unclean, impure? We simply can't. At some point in time, if we want to elevate our consciousness and rise above this material Netherland, we have to be committed to the science of spirituality, which is based in purity of thought and action. Yes, it is a struggle, but a struggle we must accept if we're to take advantage of the great gift and opportunity of the human form. If we deny the gift, we will remain a slave to the senses and run the risk of falling back into the Wheel of Transmigration.

Summarily, individuals can certainly lead whatever kind of life they choose. However, we would be wise to remember that all choices carry consequences. This book casts no judgments whatsoever. The question is, "What kind and degree of karma will such a life produce, and will that life be positively efficacious to one's spiritual ascent?"

Furthermore, will leading a casual-sex-oriented, "Free Love" life guarantee us a human life in our next birth? After all, if the primary purpose of the human form is to promote and promulgate the human species and its potential for God Realization and we do nothing to further such a Divine Realization, why should we be gifted the human form again? What positive and compelling argument can we proffer to avoid being cast down into the Wheel of Transmigration if we abuse the divinity of our human form and the rare opportunity it affords?

If people are bound to the world and its ways, they will run with the pack and manifest its consciousness. If, however, they are concerned about their existence after this life, they will focus on the type of actions and behaviors necessary to produce a positive Ascent. All roads of behavior do not move in the same direction or end at the same place. Quite to the contrary.

When the subject of promiscuous sexual behavior and the entrapping karma it produces are addressed, those individuals interested in progressing vertically on the life spectrum will be wise to focus on a life in opposition to the "Free Love" philosophy. Rather, qualities of discrimination, discernment, discipline, restraint, self-control, abstinence, chasteness, monogamy, devotion, honesty and virtue should be followed; life styles of spirituality rather than carnality adopted, and future consequences of present actions considered deeply, thoughtfully and realistically.

This chapter has served to offer food for thought in this regard. Knowing what Saints have said on the matter is an excellent guide for us all to follow as we continue our life in this incarnation.

Three takeaways from the "Free Love" philosophy which we would do well to remember are:

Promiscuity is an entrapment for the soul.

Every bonding is a binding; every coupling is a shackling.

Sexuality is an aspect of human nature not divine nature.

Richard Andrew King

CHAPTER FIVE

KARMA OF RELATIONSHIPS

The Karma of Relationships is interesting because it speaks to a reality that most people might find different from the norm. That difference is that all relationships in this world are not happenstance but predestined, pre-ordained before birth based on our past karmas.

Says Saint Charan Singh: (*Quest for Light*, p.73)

All our relationships in this world are, in fact, the adjustment of our old karmic debts. When the debtor pays off his debt, he leaves the shell immediately.

And the same thought but with a bit more information added: (Ibid., p.116)

Our marriage and all our relationships in this world are, in fact, the adjustment of our debts of karmas. When the debt is paid off, the debtor departs.

These are interesting statements because they reveal that not only our relationships but also our marriage or marriages are not happenstance but a matter of karmic reconciliation from past relationships in previous lives. This knowledge should add immense understanding to why relationships are as they are. It also makes a whole lot of sense.

Understanding this reality – that our relationships are pre-ordained – allows us to maintain a high degree of balance in life, especially when marriages fall apart and we are left wondering what happened, why they happened. It also liberates us from any sense of guilt, whether we were the individual who left the relationship or not.

There is always some external cause as to why relationships end but what appears to be the cause from a worldly point of view may not be the actual reason for the split. In fact, the real reason as to why relationships fall apart and divorces occur may be the exact opposite from what we see externally.

In truth, based on karma, we don't know the *real* reason why relationships dissolve. Things may not be as they seem at all but quite different, even totally opposite from what appears to be the worldly reason. Therefore, if we're wise, we cannot, nor should not, cast any judgements or condemnations regarding relationships for any reason.

For example, suppose one partner in a relationship just departs one day without notice or expectation, thus leaving the other partner dumbfounded and shocked. We may find fault with the one who departed. However, knowing that nothing is happenstance in this world and that karma is the underlying cause of relationships coming together or falling apart, we would be wise to look deeper and act wiser.

What if the real reason for the split was that in a previous life the one who departed had actually owed some debt to the other partner and when the debt was reconciled in this life and the karmic books balanced, the debtor left because the debt had finally been paid? Basically, the Karmic Scales of Justice had been equalized and, therefore, the relationship ended, albeit abruptly, but logically.

As Saint Charan Singh states: (Ibid., p.377)

All these worldly relationships are meant only for clearing our karmic accounts. Different persons who have karmic accounts to settle with us come into our life as our relatives, friends, acquaintances and so forth, and when their accounts are settled they drift away from us. It is our karmas that bring us together and our karmas that separate us from one another. We remain together only as long as we are destined to do so and no more. Sometimes our destiny makes us do things which are much against our wishes. We become a helpless tool in the hands of fate.

This is a powerful statement, indeed, and beautifully liberating. When we internalize the reality of relationships being predestined, we move to the center point of balance where all is calm and peaceful. If relationships or marriages come together, they were meant to come together through Karmic Law. If relationships dissolve, they were meant to do so, also by Karmic Law. To reiterate Saint Charan Singh's words:

We remain together only as long as we
are destined to do so and no more.

The obvious point regarding this discussion of relationships coming and going in our lives is that we don't know, we can't know, what the actual genesis is in any relationship or marriage. And because we can't know the facts, we can't judge and should not judge, for we have neither the right nor capacity to judge. What we witness externally may not be the actual cause of what is, and most probably is not the cause. Making allowance for this truth will go a long way to keeping us balanced, centered, calm and positive.

Knowing that all relationships are predestined, if and when they dissolve, we would be best served to understand them based on

Karmic Law and graciously let them go. We would further be wise not to engage in any manner of pejorative or negative behavior which would only be deleterious for our future and its Karmic Consequences by sowing seeds of a future negative reaping.

Understanding relationships in a worldly sense will, hopefully, allow us to focus on the one true relationship common to every human being – the divine relationship each of us has with our Creator for it is, and will always be, the primary relationship of this life or any life. Divine love, not human love, should be the primary focus of our lives. Divine love is eternal; worldly love is ephemeral. When this is realized, everything falls into place perfectly. When it is not realized, life becomes chaotic and crazy.

WORLDLY RELATIONSHIPS

Speaking of worldly relationships, Saint Jagat Singh gives us the following understanding which may well shatter our delusions about relationships.

Regarding worldly relationship, it may be pointed out that all relationships are based on selfish motives on this material plane. Husbands, brothers, wives, sisters, other relatives and friends are attached to us because of the advantages that accrue to them from us and are apt to cool down in their zeal and love towards us when they feel that we are of no use to them. Do not expect much from them but do your duty towards them and care for them even if they fail to reciprocate your love. (*The Science of the Soul*, p.135)

This passage reveals three major components of worldly relationships which can be labeled as the Egocentric Triumvirate. They are: 1. selfish motives; 2. accrual of advantage; 3. usefulness.

Such knowledge may be difficult to accept, but when we stop and reflect on our relationships in this world we see that Saint Jagat Singh is absolutely correct. Selfishly, if people have some advantage that accrues to them from knowing us, and if we are of use to them in some way, relationships may occur as far as they're concerned.

If, on the other hand, there is no advantage to others and no usefulness for them from us, what basis is there for a relationship in their minds? It's a hard truth to swallow, but true none the less. Seeing through such delusions that people love us for us only, rather than what we can do for them or how useful we are to them or what advantages accrue to them from us, is liberating and allows us to focus on the one true relationship that is eternally enduring – our relationship with God, with the Creator.

Can we prove this reality of worldly relationships being based on selfishness, accrual of advantage and usefulness? Yes. All we have to do is reflect on why people are connected to us. The answer and its truth will be obvious.

To be clear, though, not every relationship in the world can be characterized as a "worldly relationship" per se. There are relationships in this world that are extremely spiritual. These are manifested when the consciousness of the parties involved is mutually based in spiritual principles of godliness, morality, purity of conduct, selfless and ethical behavior devoid of the three factors mentioned above - selfish motives, accrual of advantage and usefulness. Saints, for example, although living in the world, involve themselves with individuals and their disciples but their connection is one of supernal selflessness, spirituality and love, never worldliness, carnality or usury.

What is meant by "worldly relationships" are those personal associations saturated in material and carnal desires, as well as the Egocentric Triumvirate.

On the other hand, spiritual relationships involve the *highest and best good* of each partner. Using someone or our relationship with them merely for selfish purposes or accruing some advantage from them is not, repeat not, in their highest and best good. Therefore, lying, cheating stealing, ridiculing, denigrating, disparaging, demeaning, deceiving or destroying someone or their reputation is not an integral aspect of a spiritual relationship. Worldly relationships may engage in all the aforementioned negative acts. In contrast, spiritual relationships are based on true love, and love only gives, not takes. Love never calculates some advantage. Love simply loves and holds in its heart the highest and best good of everyone - their wholeness, sanctity, freedom, health, well-being, success and happiness.

Richard Andrew King

For most of us who are seeking to climb the Divine Ladder, we exhibit both worldly and spiritual energies. As we continue on the Spiritual Path, however, the material mindset and consciousness ultimately give way to the spiritual mindset and consciousness until the latter completely absorbs us and is reflected in our character and lifestyle. Such a process involves a life-long, or lives-long, journey of transiting from the material and carnal to the spiritual and ethereal; from usury and denigration to love and edification.

Should we be concerned or worried about such a transition? No. Such a transformation naturally takes time. None of us is perfect and we need time to change.

As Saint Charan Singh notes: (*Quest for Light*, Letter #387)

Our destiny is all marked out and we have to reap what we have sown, then why worry? Face life cheerfully, doing the best you can under the circumstances and then leaving the rest to the Lord.

One of the problems most of us humans have is that we tend to be social creatures and the transition between a worldly existence of total sociability to a spiritual life primarily requiring solitude and independence for purposes of thought, meditation, reflection and introspection can be challenging. But not to worry. If we are meant to follow the Spiritual Path, we will naturally resonate with its requirements and lifestyle. The spiritual journey is about reversing the outward flow of our consciousness to an inward flow where we can connect with the internal energies of Spirit. When the time is right, we will feel right at home in not only making but embracing such a change and transition.

In this regard, Saint Charan Singh remarks:

Our problem is that we always love the company of others; we don't love our own company at all . . . We don't try to live with ourselves at all. We must learn to live with ourselves, independently of anything in this world. (Newsletter, 10/2004)

Additionally, if we are drawn to the Spiritual Path it will be because of our karmas from previous lives, so we have no need to worry about a thing. In fact, people who are making the transition from a material to a spiritual journey will be comfortable with being independent, alone, solitary. How else can one turn off the outward flow of one's consciousness? As Saint Charan Singh succinctly says in *The Master Answers*: (Radha Soami Satsang Beas, Punjab, India, 5th edition, 1980, Answer #370)

Karma will take care of our choice automatically.

In fact, he states emphatically: (Ibid., Answer #609)

Nothing happens without karma.

To solidify Karmic Reality, he notes: (Ibid., Answer #472)

Karma – nobody can escape, whether one believes it or not.

And as far as coming to the Spiritual Path is concerned, he asserts: (Ibid., Answer #421)

Actually, one who is to come to the Path
is being guided right from the beginning.

Therefore, the issue of us making a transition from a worldly life to a divine life will happen if it's destined to be so. Our primary focus in relationship should be to be the giver, not the taker; to strive for the highest and best good of everyone with whom we are in relationship and not to be a user or manipulator for our personal advantage. We must never forget that what we sow, we reap, and we cannot reap what we do not sow. If we take the high road of truly being the giver and avoid the low road of being the taker, we'll either pay off old karmic debts and/or generate good karmas going forward.

RELATIONSHIPS - GOOD OR BAD?

In this duality-based world, everything has two sides - one positive, one negative. So it is with relationships. But what is interesting is that what we consider a bad relationship may not only be good but a blessing in disguise.

The ultimate purpose of being human is to reunite our souls with the Creator, i.e., merge our drop of divine energy with the ocean of God's energy. In order to do this we have to redirect our attention *inward* toward our spiritual center and away from the *outward* domain of the material/carnal world. As long as our attention and focus is on the *outward*, we cannot move inward. It's impossible. Therefore, if we're involved in a "bad" relationship that keeps us engaged externally and does nothing to fulfill our happiness, peace and well-being, we may have to redirect our energy inward to seek that Power which does fulfill us, which gives us peace and purpose.

It's no secret that in order to redirect our life focus inwardly, God may make us uncomfortable, unsatisfied and unfulfilled with our worldly life to force us inward. After all, if we are completely happy with our worldly life, why would we ever turn inward? We wouldn't. This is why so many people find God during the dark times of their lives rather than in their moments of joy, happiness and fulfillment. Bad, negative or disruptive relationships are one method designed to redirect our attention inwardly to achieve this end.

Richard Andrew King

Therefore, bad relationships or marriages may be more of a blessing than a curse. The most important aspect of this human life is not to indulge solely in the pleasures and pursuits of the world but to use them to merge with that Force that is our natural divine heritage and Home. In this case, the means may well justify the ends.

Furthermore, it may not be a bad relationship that forces us to rethink our life's purpose and direction of movement. It could be hardship or adversity of any kind of intensity such as disease, poverty, loneliness, emptiness, pain, sorrow, suffering. All of these so-called "bad things" may, in fact, be good things. Therefore, when we're assailed with any problem in life, we would be wise to ask, "Where's the blessing?" Remember, every coin has two sides, so there must be a positive side to any negative experience. We just have to look for it. It has to be there.

This said, whatever our karma is in this life, we should not decry it, rant or rail against it but embrace it, work with it and actually give thanks for it. After all, we created it and, therefore, must take responsibility for it. This is the Karmic Algorithm. Remember the drumbeat?

We reap what we sow and we cannot
reap what we do not sow.

Whatever we are reaping now,
we ourselves have sewn before.

What we put onto the circle of life
circles back to encircle us.

The sower of the poison cannot but
be engulfed in the poison.

The fruit of action unfailingly
overtakes the doer.

Be not deceived; God is not mocked: for
whatsoever a man soweth, that shall he also reap.

This is Karmic Law and it is the truth of this world.

Richard Andrew King

WE REAP THE DEEDS

We reap the deeds of the seeds we've sown.
We harvest the fruit of the fruit we've grown.
It's axiomatic, we must atone
for every act that is our own.

No one escapes this Karmic Law.
Why don't we, then, proclaim its awe?
Instead, we live as blind outlaw,
thinking we can beat the Law.

How many times must we be told
of this Primal Law forever old?
How ignorant, arrogant, sad and bold
that we must constantly be retold

that we reap the deeds of the seeds we've sown;
We harvest the fruit of the fruit we've grown?
It's axiomatic, we must atone
for every act that is our own.

Rest assured, this Law is true.
It governs gods. It governs you.
It governs every minute thing you do,
and constantly will follow you

throughout your lives in countless forms;
through quiet meadows and vicious storms;
through hells and heavens and cruciforms –
everything conforms.

Until we rise above the Pair,
we have no power to forswear
this Law which governs every hair
on every head both foul and fair.

We reap the deeds of the seeds we've sown.
We harvest the fruit of the fruit we've grown.
It's axiomatic, we must atone
for every act that is our own.

MORALITY

Morality is not an end
but a means to gain His Favor.
If we choose Liberation,
then His Purity we must savor.

He's the One who holds the key.
Our souls are in His Trust.
If it's Salvation we desire,
then His Morality's a must.

Purity of action
and purity of thought
gain us recognition
and dispensation for our Lot.

Not to court His wishes,
will never make us free.
Once, again, we must realize –
He's the One who holds *the* Key.

There isn't any other way
to escape this prison and its walls.
If we don't follow Him
and His Commands and Morals,

then we will just stay put,
a prisoner in the realm
of blind, enshrouding darkness
with the Devil at the helm.

The dictates and beliefs
of the masses bear no weight.
When it comes to Liberation,
God's the Keeper of His Gate.

No one leaves this world
defying *the* Trustee.
It's permanent imprisonment
or His Morality.

CHAPTER SIX

KARMA OF DIET

Diet – what we physically consume for our sustenance, health and pleasure – is one of the most critical aspects of pursuing a spiritual life, more than is universally known or understood. If we're not concerned with moving up in the Hierarchy of Consciousness and remaining in this dark and nether world via the Wheel of Transmigration, then diet will be of little to no concern for us. However, if we want to continue our ascent beyond the human rung of the evolutionary ladder, we must regard our diet and its karmic ramifications as a fundamental imperative without contention.

What we put into our bodies has a direct effect not only on our physical well-being but also on our spiritual advancement. In order to merge our soul back into the Divine Ocean of God's energy, our energy must be pure and devoid of all karmic bonds, both negative and positive. Our diet has a direct bearing on the purity of our energy and consciousness.

VEGETARIAN DIET

To the end of purifying our energy and neutralizing our karma, a vegetarian diet is absolutely requisite. As Saint Jagat Singh states: (*The Science of the Soul*, p.171)

So long as one does not give up the animal diet,
one cannot begin the Spiritual Journey.

Here's why. The answer of living by a vegetarian diet is very simple and explained by Saint Charan Singh: (*The Master Answers*, p.298)

We must follow it. There is no other way for spiritual progress . . . If we kill, we will be killed. We should never forget that. Christ said, "Love thy neighbor." All creatures are our neighbors . . . When you love anybody, you do not kill that individual, and when we love the whole creation, we cannot kill intentionally, nor could we find it in our heart to have it done for us by someone else.

This fundamental spiritual admonition is clearly stated as the Sixth Commandment in the Bible: (King James Version, Exodus 20:13)

Thou shalt not kill.

The Clarion Karmic Call of sowing and reaping couldn't be more clear or simple. We sow, we reap, and if we sow killing we insure that we will be killed. That's the Karmic Algorithm. Subsequently, our karmic debt created in killing is extremely heavy and burdensome, interfering with our ability to be pure in consciousness and therefore negating our climb up the spiritual ladder.

But John Doe queries, "What's the difference between killing animals or killing vegetables and fruits? We're still killing, right?" The answer is, "Yes, we're still killing, but the amount of spiritual substance in the plant kingdom is far less than that in the animal, fish, aves or even insect kingdoms, so our karmic debt is much less severe and easier to pay off. It's the difference between a blade of grass and an animal, the latter's consciousness is far higher and therefore its destruction carries greater karmic debt. Thus, Saints recommend eating plants and fruits whose killing involves the least amount of negative karma. The less karma, the less debt, the faster the ascent.

Saint Charan Singh explains further in the following quotations: (Ibid., p.297)

Life has to live on life, so the Saints advise us to collect the least amount of karma while living in this world, and for that reason they advise us to live on fruits and vegetables.

In *Quest for Light* he reminds us: (Letter #193)

Non-vegetarian food means an extremely heavy karmic debt which is very difficult to pay.

And: (Ibid., Letter #204)

The food we eat produces a great effect upon our mind. 'As we eat, so our mind becomes' is an old saying and a very true one. Bad food gives rise to bad thoughts. Pure food will encourage pure thoughts. Pure thoughts will create good character and good character is most essential for love of God.

And: (Ibid., Letter #204)

Where is the need of killing birds, fish and animals and making our body a graveyard? The human body, in which the Lord resides and which is the only specie in which He can be realized, should be kept as pure and clean as possible.

It is a great sin . . . to take any life and then satisfy our appetite with that flesh. You yourself may not be doing the actual killing but that makes little difference.

The Bible echoes the principle of vegetarianism. (Genesis 1: 29)

And God said, Behold, I have given you every herb bearing seed, which is upon the face of all the earth, and every tree, in the which is the fruit of a tree yielding seed; to you it shall be for meat.

To be direct, murderous winds of action bring murderous winds of reaction. Poisonous seed gives poisonous fruit. Killing begets killing. Suffering begets suffering. Such is Karmic Law and it is inescapable.

FAMOUS VEGETARIANS

There are and have been many famous individuals throughout history who have preached vegetarianism. Following are a few quotes from some of them.

George Bernard Shaw was an Irish playwright and the leading dramatist of his time. He also won the Nobel Prize for Literature in 1925. Of vegetarianism, he said:

Animals are my friends . . . and I don't eat my friends.

And . . .

We are the living graves of murdered beasts, slaughtered to satisfy our appetites.

Not exactly a complimentary or wholesome description, is it – humans being the living graves of murdered beasts slaughtered to satisfy their appetites? Nor does it speak well of humans and our level of spiritual awareness and consciousness which, by consuming flesh, inescapably validates our material and carnal mindset.

Mohandas Gandhi, the famous Indian leader, stated:

I do not regard flesh-food as necessary for us at any stage and under any clime in which it is possible for human beings ordinarily to live. I hold flesh-food to be unsuited to our species. We err in copying the lower animal world – if we are superior to it.

Nobel Peace Prize Laureate Dr. Albert Schweitzer (1952) was a famous humanitarian, theologian, philosopher, writer, physician and organist noted for his "Reverence for Life" philosophy. Dr. Schweitzer commented:

Until he extends the circle of his compassion to all living things, man will not himself find peace.

Dr. Albert Einstein was the greatest scientist of the 20th Century, Nobel Laureate for Physics in 1921, and Time Magazine's Person of the Century. He noted:

Nothing will benefit human health and increase the chances for survival of life on earth as much as the evolution to a vegetarian diet.

Buddha observes:

To become vegetarian is to step into the stream which leads to nirvana.

So compassion and love for others, even animals, fish, birds, etc., is a major foundation stone of vegetarianism. But as Saints teach, the negative karma accumulated through the consumption of flesh is hazardous to our spiritual progress because it shackles us to this world, to a consciousness that is both material and carnal.

How can we possibly ascend to more ethereal states of being, which is the gift and purpose of being graced with a human body, when we're chained to this dense, dark and heavy world? We can't. It's indefensible logic. When we kill, we will be killed. Killing others in this world means we will be forced to stay here to reconcile our karma of killing.

Therefore, living a vegetarian lifestyle cuts the Karmic Killing Cycle, allowing us to not accumulate more dense, enslaving and enshackling karma prohibiting our ascent. Simply put, by eating flesh we enslave ourselves to this world. If we want out of this lurid labyrinthine prison, then we have no choice but to live by a vegetarian diet.

Saint Dariya of Bihar lived in the 17th/18th Centuries. He asserts: (*Dariya Sahib – Saint of Bihar*, K.N. Upadhyaya, Radha Soami Satsang Beas, 1987, 1st edition, p.372)

One incurs an enormous sin by killing a single living being . . .
Just as our own life is dear to us, so is life
dear to all other beings.

Dariya spares no boldness when he says this: (Ibid., p.374)

The deluded one who perpetrates bloodshed will find his way to the door of hell. He who kills an animal and eats it will soon go to hell. Whatever good or evil deeds one performs, one has to face the result. Only a kind-hearted one is said to go to heaven.

And he doesn't stop there. He continues: (Ibid., p.375)

Reflect and be sympathetic to the pain of living beings; recognize the nature of pain by looking within your own self.

And . . .

Knowing your own child to be happy, you embrace him with delight. But you peel off the skin of others, for which you will suffer the same fate.

And . . .

When you see others in pain, you rejoice and feel greatly delighted. But it will recoil and fall on you, bringing you similar pain and suffering.

And: (Ibid., p.377)

Shedding of others' blood is paid for with one's own blood. Such is the law. Take this to heart, says Dariya.

And: (Ibid., p.383)

If you have no compassion in your heart, you are indeed seeking disaster. You will suffer many dips in the ocean of the world.

And finally, a five word directive: (Ibid., p.384)

Never take meat and fish.

We could easily fill an entire book of such quotations. Yet, how often in today's modern, "civilized," technologically developed world do we ever hear these truths? Answer: never, and that's a massive problem as far as our spiritual well-being is concerned. It further explains why this world is so dark, even evil. Time and time again, as we delve into the reality of this world, we find these great truths which serve as a guiding light, not just to this life but to our very existence. "But why," we ask, "have such truths been suppressed in the first place, and who's responsible for the suppression?" This is the exact reason why we need to think for ourselves, act on our own instincts and common sense and always question the status quo.

TYPES OF VEGETARIANISM

By definition vegetarians do not eat flesh of any kind – no meat, fish or fowl. If someone says they're a vegetarian but still eats fish, they're not a vegetarian. They are a pescatarian – one who is partially vegetarian but eats fish and seafood. But fish flesh is still flesh and comes with karmic chains and shackles. Saints advise us to not eat any flesh whatsoever, as Saint Dariya stated above.

The three major types of vegetarians are vegan, lacto and ovo-lacto. Vegans consume no animal products whatsoever.

Lacto-vegetarians allow milk and non-animal-based rennet in their diet. Rennet, normally found in cheese products, is derived from the stomach linings of calves and young animals, so it is forbidden. However, plant-based rennet and microbial rennet are safe to consume.

Ovo-lacto vegetarians allow eggs and egg whites in their diet. Saints recommend a vegan or lacto-vegetarian diet but disallow eggs because of their embryonic nature. Plus, eggs are a dense food and are derived from the lower chakras (energy vortexes) of the body.

PLEASURE POISONS

Pleasure Poisons include alcohol, recreational drugs and nicotine products. People will argue for their beer, wine, marijuana and cigarettes but each of these substances interferes with the soul's ability to connect with the energy of Spirit, thus blocking and barring spiritual ascent. They have no part in a spiritual diet or lifestyle.

Furthermore, misuse and overuse of these Pleasure Poisons can cause massive problems in one's life, adding more negative karma to one's debt structure. But because these substances are an integral part of the material/carnal world, people will argue for them, cling to them, support them. This is natural for worldly-minded souls, but the truth is that they are still poisons because they poison our ability to go Within and connect with the finer energies of God, and unless we connect with His energies, which are totally pure, we will not be able to make spiritual gains or escape from this nether land.

Alcohol, recreational drugs and nicotine products are material by definition and by resonating with the world's material energy they keep us trapped in a material environment, negating any spiritual progress. People may argue for them all day long, all life long, but their protestations and argumentations will be of no avail. Spirit resonates with Spirit, not matter. If it is a spiritual life we desire, then we must live a life of spirit, not matter.

Furthermore, just think of all the problems these Pleasure Poisons create, problems generating more, even massive, karmic debts, destruction and disease. How many lives have been damaged through the use of alcohol and drugs? How many deaths have occurred because of them? How many families and relationships have suffered as a result of alcohol and drug abuse? How many diseases have resulted because of them? How many bad and regretful decisions have been made under their influence?

If we want a healthy, whole, happy life, these Pleasure Poisons of alcohol, recreational drugs and nicotine products must be avoided. If we choose to follow the Spiritual Path, we have no choice but to disallow these insidious substances in our life. They inhibit our upward progress, potentially cause problems and deny us a positively wholesome life. Saints disallow them and so must we if we seek to rise above and beyond this world. There is no compromise. They must be expelled; their use denied.

In summation, the best diet we can have in this world, if we choose to follow a spiritual lifestyle, is a vegetarian diet devoid of the Pleasure Poisons of alcohol, recreational drugs and nicotine. Following a non-vegetarian diet and using any or all of the Pleasure Poisons creates extraordinary degrees of negative karma which are extremely difficult to pay off, i.e., to neutralize, not to mention the problems they create in the normal process of living.

What we put into our bodies indeed makes a huge difference, not only in the quality of our present life but also of those lives still to come. But what kind of lives will those be? That's the question.

The human body is the greatest gift any soul can have. It and it alone allows us the divine capacity of not only knowing of God but merging our soul into His Soul. If we keep the body pure, our journey ahead will be positive. However, if we choose to defile our body with killing and death then we will have no one to blame but ourselves when our heads are on the chopping block. We sow, we reap, and we cannot reap what we do not sow. This is Karmic Law and it is *the* Law of this world.

ANIMAL FOOD

© Richard Andrew King

Animal food to animal plane;
omnivorous diet, dangerous game.
We cannot ascend to spiritual planes
when slaughtering animals for selfish gains.

The Way of the Spirit is Spirit true.
Consuming flesh will consume you.
Negative karma do we accrue
when we the carcass of animals chew.

Forever will we be forlorn
when we our heads with flesh adorn.
Forever will we have to morn
for eating those of mother born.

Personal choice is fine to make
but it would be a grave mistake
to think our deeds the Law forsakes
when we the lives of creatures take.

No one escapes the act of killing.
No one thought perhaps more chilling
than paying recompense for the filling
of our bowels with the blood we're spilling.

Consider why the world suffers.
Slaughtering children of their mothers
and eating their flesh most surely colors
the karmas we reap from eating others.

The Law exonerates no woman, man
for eating the flesh of children.
Celebrity, pontiff, pauper, king –
no absolution for murdering.

Critical to Freedom, this feeding game;
'tis but ourselves we have to blame
when we cannot our diets tame;
our lot—to suffer just the same.

Think you'll escape? Think again!
Consuming flesh is tragic sin.
Horrific penalties accrue to him
or her who is not vegetarian.

CITY OF THE DEAD

Awake! Awake! Dear Soul, awake!
Shake loose the slumber from your head.
This world, this residence we claim,
Remains the City of the Dead.
Where'er we move, step, eat or sleep;
What'er profess in discourse deep,
We cannot lose the death we keep.
Blind poor wretched souls are we.

How vile, how false our every breath.
We love to live but live on death.
In spite of all our honest willing,
We cannot reconcile the killing.
And so, in weakness, turn blinded eye.
Yet, all that lives must live to die.
Oh, the karma on our head
To love this City of the Dead.

Cold-hearted butchers cast in stone,
A title we would never own;
But, yet, when we dead carcass crave,
Our forms become a living grave
For all the souls we blindly killed
Just to have our stomachs filled.

'Tis us, poor creatures, we should dread
To claim this City of the Dead.

Amazingly, we have no guilt
For all the living blood we've spilt.
Think we not of all the pain
We inflict for selfish gain
On all those creatures we have slain?
How could we ever think we're sane?
Could we not eat plants instead
Of gorging on the slaughtered dead?

We justify each and every blow
We wield to kill another soul.
'Tis only our debased opinion –
We think, when God gave man dominion,
He meant for us to harm and kill
All other creatures for our will.
Oh, lethal karma on our head,
For living thoughts of living dead.

Awake! Awake! Dear Soul, awake!
Your killing sets the seed,
And all your senseless slaughter
and rapacious, carnal greed
will, one day, come returning
against your fervent will

Richard Andrew King

making you the dinner
of some creature and its kill.
You think you will escape the Law –

Pshaw!

To slaughter animals and steal their breath
Gnaw on their bones and chew their flesh,
And slurp their blood with frenzied zeal
Reaps torturous horror on the Wheel.*
Except, if we be ever bright,
And waken from this carnal night,
We may begin to cut the web
And leave this City of the Dead.

But such behavior butts the horns
Of all those creatures in human form
Who live to slaughter, maim and kill
And sanctify their petty will.
Awake, Dear Soul, and know this Truth –
Eating flesh with human tooth
Will guarantee that you be fed
To other forms when you are dead.

Therefore,

Awake! Awake! His Truth do dread,
It governs this City of the Dead;
And of all the laws forever true,
Make no mistake, it governs you!

*Wheel of Transmigration

Richard Andrew King

CHAPTER SEVEN

KARMA OF ABORTION

Abortion is defined as the termination of a pregnancy resulting in the death of a fetus; in human terms, a child. To abort or not to abort has always been controversial between those who believe in the fetus's *right to life* (pro-life) versus those who believe in a woman's *right to choose* (pro-choice). This chapter offers information which may allow individuals to make a more sentient and judicious decision regarding abortion.

Abortion is a matter of personal choice. As aforesaid, God does not disallow us from making choices, but He also does not disallow us from experiencing the consequences of those choices. In fact, experiencing the consequences of our choices is mandated by Karmic Law. What we sow, we reap and we cannot reap what we do not sow. It is this aspect of the abortion argument that is addressed here.

To the point, Karmic Law says that if we abort a fetus, we will be aborted in some future birth at some future time. What goes around, comes around. There is no escaping this reality. However, when is this "future" aspect of the abortion debate ever discussed? Answer: Up to now, never.

The entire abortion argument of today (21st Century) exists only in the present tense, in a carnal sense, but never in the future tense with a spiritual sense. Ergo, the "present tense perspective" of abortion is extremely myopic. Rather, the "future tense perspective" should be given maximum consideration because the consequences of the "present tense" version are horrific, to say the least.

ABORTION TIMING & ARGUMENTS

One of the main arguments in the abortion debate is the timing of an abortion. The *Pro-life* side says that life begins with conception; the *Pro-choice* side says abortion, even post-birth infanticide, is justified.

Arguments for abortion are varied and many but their focus is always on the rights of the woman but never on the rights of the unborn living fetus. The timing and arguments for or against abortion, however, are inconsequential from a karmic perspective. Here's why.

When we strike a match, a flame is created. It has been given a life of its own. As fuel and oxygen are added to the fire of the flame, the flame grows. How big it grows is the question. If the flame is extinguished, even in the first micro-second of its existence, it will die. In effect, the flame was aborted and no fire, however large or grand, could exist.

The point is that when the match was struck and the flame ignited but subsequently extinguished, the flame was *denied the process of life*. It is the same with human abortion. When a fetus is aborted, the soul created in that instant of conception, just like the match flame, is denied the *process of life* and it is this *denial of the process of life*, especially human life, that is the fundamental karmic issue of abortion. When we deny life, life will be denied to us, eventually.

What does this mean? It means that those who abort a fetus are denying to that soul the Flame of Life and the process of growing and evolving. Therefore, at some future time in some potential life, the "aborter" will be denied the Flame of Life and the process of evolving.

When we deny, we will be denied; when we abort, we will be aborted; when we kill, we must be killed. This is Karmic Law, and no one escapes it, regardless of the litany of arguments made in the defense of abortion. Yes, the aborter has the right to choose, but actions intrinsically carry the exact consequences of their genesis. Remember these quotes?

Whatever you have sewn, the same shall you reap.
No change in this shall there ever be.
~ Saint Ravidas

Be not deceived; God is not mocked: for
whatsoever a man soweth, that shall he also reap.
~ Bible – Galatians 6:7

Whatever we are reaping now,
we ourselves have sewn before.
~ Saint Sawan Singh

What we put onto the circle of life
circles back to encircle us.
~ King

None of us can escape the reality of Karmic Law, which transcends human law. We can make all the arguments we want for abortion in the court of worldly laws, but it is the court of Karmic Law that determines consequences.

Furthermore, we must never forget that the human form is the Crown Jewel, the Top of the Ladder, of living beings in this world.

When we abort a child, we are denying that soul the greatest gift of life in this creation – the potential of not only knowing there's a God but the ultimate attainment of merging our soul with the Soul of the Creator. When we engage in the process of conceiving a child, we are playing our part in the spiritual development of that soul. How important is that? Answer: massively important. However, when we deny a soul the right to a divine life, then how ignoble, how selfish, how tragic is that? Answer: massively important, not just for the unborn child being denied a human birth, but more so for the "aborter," whose future will be one of being aborted.

Often overlooked in the abortion debate is the fact that although we say our bodies belong to us, in reality they do not. Our human body is on loan to us temporarily to experience the potential it offers for spiritual advancement. Frankly, we do not own our body, so any arguments relating to the body are invalid prima facie.

Furthermore, a major component of the abortion decision should contain a deliberation of the ramifications of the principles of transmigration and reincarnation. As Saint Charan Singh reminds us:

The human body is not given to us in every birth. We get it only after millions of lives, and it is a very rare and precious gift not to be wasted upon the perishable things and objects of this world.

Thus, the question remains, "What are we going to do in this life to guarantee we receive a human body in our next life rather than being thrown back into the Wheel of Transmigration where we may be forced to live millions of lives in sub-human species before we are graced with a human body again, if at all?" Certainly, this concept has never been discussed in the abortion debate. Yet, it is, or should be, intrinsically major to the debate, if not the primary focus of the debate.

When we abort a child, we are not only denying life to that soul but potentially setting the stage for our sub-human existence in the Wheel of Transmigration. After all, if we deny a soul the right to the greatest living form in this creation, i.e., the human form, why should we be granted such a gift in the future? If we deny human life, then human life will be denied to us. We sow, we reap and we cannot reap what we do not sow. The drumbeat rolls on.

Now, the argument can be made that if we abort a child it was in the karma of that soul to be aborted. True, but our own decision to abort will only continue the cycle for us. The best choice is to make the divine choice – grant the incoming soul the opportunity of a human body. In such a case, both the incoming soul and the mother will be blessed and any negative karmic effects avoided.

ABORTION ALTERNATIVES

So, what's the alternative to abortion? If the child is not wanted by the natural birth mother or father, the simple answer is to give the baby up for adoption, which is a far wiser and more spiritual solution than abortion. Still, we must note that if we "give away" we will eventually be "given away."

There are adults, both women and men, who are interested in adopting a child or children for any number of reasons. Why not give them a chance to do so? Also, there exist private charitable organizations in which the infant can be placed. The reality is that abortion does not have to occur. Alternatives do exist, and for the spiritual welfare of both the birth mother and father, as well as the incoming soul, adoption is a viable solution.

OUR LIFE, OUR RESPONSIBILITY

In spite of any debate regarding abortion, the fact remains that this is Our Life and it is Our Responsibility. There is no one else who is responsible for our choices in life - no government, no organization, no family or friends. Just us. We are the ones who ultimately have to pay the price for our actions, who have to live the consequences of our choices and no one else.

The basic purpose of sex is to procreate and promulgate human existence. If we engage in sexual actions, then we must accept the consequences of those actions, whether positive or negative. If a child is naturally conceived in the process of sex, then we must not forsake the child or abdicate our responsibility to the incoming soul. If we do renounce our responsibility for reasons of inconvenience, pleasure, having to raise a child with all of its attendant responsibilities, etc., then we're acting selfishly and irresponsibly. We are not owning up to our duties as one to whom an incoming soul was divinely given. If effect, we have not only aborted the child, we have aborted our own responsibility, and the last thing we should want to do as a mature, whole, intelligent, spiritual adult is to turn our back on life, which includes our own future lives.

In summation, when the circumstance of abortion presents itself, we would be wise to consider the spiritual ramifications rather than simple worldly solutions. The consequences of abortion from a spiritual point of view are massive. Denying an incoming soul the opportunity of experiencing the benefits of a human body is egregious and portends that we, by Karmic Law, will eventually be denied the greatest of all gifts in this creation – the gift of a human form and its opportunity of not only knowing God but of potentially being able to merge our energy back into His and escape from the prison of this world. No other living form of the 8,400,000 forms in the Wheel of Transmigration is given this prodigious privilege except man, and when man denies such an incredible gift to another through the process of abortion, he walks along a narrow plank of losing his step and falling into a foreboding and dark existence. As Guru Nanak warned us:

The cycle of transmigration is dreadful
and it is beyond the comprehension of
the human intellect.

The bottom line, of course, is that each person must choose for himself or herself whether to engage in abortion or not, but whatever the choice is, the consequences of that choice cannot be avoided. If we sow death by abortion, we will reap death by abortion. If we sow life, then life, especially human life, may well be granted to us going forward. The choice is ours, and the wise choice of granting life is definitely the right choice relative to our future existence.

Richard Andrew King

HUMAN BIRTH

© Richard Andrew King

Human birth is critical
to the journey of the soul.
Our actions taken day by day
determine where we go
when the current lifetime ends
and its karmas all wrap up.
Do we descend to deeper depths,
or do we journey Up?

If the Journey can progress,
it can regress as well.
If the soul can rise to Heaven,
it can surely fall to Hell.
If we can take a forward step,
we can, as well, fall back.
How critical is this human birth
to keep us on His Track?

Just because we're human
doesn't mean we gain
a human birth forever,
so we must seek to tame
the impulses and instincts
which trap us in the Wheel,

and keep us from advancing
to Divinity's Ideal.

It won't be long before our days
come, sadly, to an end.
And who knows just how long
the time will be 'til then?
Tomorrow or the next day?
We never know the When
of the Reaper's Deadly coming
when he wields his scythe again.

Therefore, it is critical
for us to mind the store,
for the actions that we make today
may bind us evermore
to life upon the Wheel
and rounds of living hell,
or life within His Light Domain
where Life is ever Well.

ABORTION

© Richard Andrew King

God gave us life; we ask not why,
so who are we to life deny?
What rights have we to take a knife
preempting souls their right to life?

Convenience, pleasure – is this our goal
as we forfeit the life of another soul?
How can we truly justify the cost,
especially when a child's life is lost?

We claim we have the right to choose
in any way this life to use.
Really? Are we satisfied
that such a right is justified?

To take a life is clearly sin,
and what goes 'round comes back again,
so next time 'round what is our chance
of escaping abortion's consequence?

If we abort a child today
eventually, we will have to pay.
What will the price at that time be?
That's right. Abortion is the guarantee.

Therefore, giving birth is the only choice
to allow a child its human voice,
so next time we will have the chance
of a human life in which to dance.

Thus, will Grace be on our head
for loving life and not the dead.
In giving life to an inbound soul
our gracious gift will make us whole

Preventing us from being sent
into the Wheel where life is spent
transiting endless sub-human forms
blind, forsaken and forlorn.

CHAPTER EIGHT

KARMA OF POWER

Arguably, the Karma of Power is the most blessed or cursed type of karma because of the magnification of the power, either negative or positive. Additionally, power in itself is highly seductive and alluring. When associated with one of the Five Hindrances (Pride, Anger, Greed, Attachment, Lust) power becomes extremely dangerous.

As Lord Acton famously wrote to Archbishop Mandell Creighton on 5 April 1887: (Online Library of Liberty)

Power tends to corrupt, and absolute power corrupts absolutely.
Great men are almost always bad men.

Such a statement is, obviously, a harsh indictment for anyone holding the mantle of power in any profession, job, organization, government, company, church, media, business, university, etc. Such souls walk on a razor's edge where the potential of generating massive negative karma is a distinct possibility. Yet, as we look at leaders in general, the overwhelming number of them seem to be quite indifferent, oblivious, even blind to the karmic ramifications of their actions. Hence, such souls should be extremely judicious in the exercise of their power.

Eighteenth Century British poet, Thomas Gray, shares this thought from his famous poem, *Elegy Written in a Country Churchyard,* published in 1751.

The boast of heraldry, the pomp of power,
and all that beauty, all that wealth e're gave,
awaits alike the inevitable hour.
The paths of glory lead but to the grave.

This quatrain reminds us of this simple truth – that no matter how high our station in life the grave is our final destination. But more to the point, for those who misuse their power, the grave may last forever. Here's why. The following analogy is simple and somewhat crude but instructive nonetheless.

Man #1 tells a lie, one lie, to Man #2 who suffers for one year because of Man #1's lie. Because karma returns to us the same energy and its manifestation that we placed onto the circle of life,

Man #1, by telling such a lie, guarantees himself one year of suffering in his future for the suffering he caused to Man #2.

Now here's the rub. Let's say Man #1 occupies a position of high governmental power. He repeats the same injurious lie he told Man #2 to 300,000,000 (three hundred million) people who also individually suffer for one year because of the lie. Thus, Man #1, by telling such a lie, may well have to suffer for 300,000,000 years – the amount of time involved in the aggregate suffering of those to whom he lied, and all because of one lie! This is the danger of power! How many lives in how many forms in how many eons of time will it take for Man #1 to pay off his karmic debt of injuring 300,000,000 souls? Perhaps this is one reason Saint Charan Singh said:

The human body is not given to us in every birth.
We get it only after millions of lives.

And remember, all this negative karma was generated from just one lie. How is the position of power looking now? How seductive? How alluring? How self-aggrandizing? How troubling? How burdensome? How precarious? How dangerous? How critical?

Power is a perilous attribute, as the analogy above reveals. One lie, just one, can cause untold misery for untold periods of time to untold numbers of people. Yet, how many lies do people in power tell on a moment-to-moment, day-to-day basis? How many lies do we tell? How much suffering and turmoil result in lies? How much karma have we created for ourselves when we lie, especially as a leader?

Negative karma doesn't have to be associated just with a lie. It can be any category of action that harms others or even one's self. The concerning factor is that individuals in a power or leadership position have wide ranging influence over many people. Any and every decision or action they make or take will affect countless individuals and potentially their families. This is why the Karma of Power is so dangerous - it has wide reaching depths and dimensions.

Creating an action the size of a camp fire is quite different from that of a forest fire. People in power can create a forest fire with one simple action, and here's the rub for them: the rebounding karma will be equal to the original action. Camp fires can be soothing and enjoyable but forest fires have massive destructive capability. It's easy to put out a camp fire, but a forest fire? Not so easy. Quite to the contrary.

So here's a question that we or any person in a power position have to ask. "Are we willing to experience the same type and degree of suffering we cause to others through our actions and decisions?" We won't, can't, escape our karma. It will eventually rebound upon us. We reap what we sow and we cannot reap what we do not sow. The greater the power, the greater the sowing; the greater the reaping; the greater the suffering. So how will we act? Likewise, however, the sowing of goodness will return goodness to us as a matter of Karmic Law. Hopefully, our lives are lived with this positive purpose rather than its opposite.

If we think this scenario of rebounding karma is without merit, we should ask ourselves why we suffer in the first place. Saints tell us that our diseases, sufferings, sorrows, hardships, etc., are karmic manifestations of our own past actions and will pass when the karmic debt is paid.

Says Saint Sawan Singh: (*Divine Light*, pp.77 and 195)

Disease comes to us as a result of our past actions and disappears when it has done its work.

It is needless for me to repeat that disease is caused by past karma and it goes away when the karma has been undergone.

From *Spiritual Gems*, he states: (Letter #70)

Suffering and poverty are also pre-ordained for everyone before his birth according to the karma of his past birth.

And: (Ibid., Letter #144)

Disease is due to karma . . . through disease the bad karma is being fulfilled. Disease is the unloading of the burden and paying off the debt.

As we follow the Spiritual Path we will begin to evaluate our every action and its potential consequence, as well we should. Nothing is happenstance in our lives. We create our own destiny. By being ethical, honest and pure in thought, word and action while in the present life, we design our future life and lives in a positive way.

As 18th/19th Century German dramatist, poet and historian Friedrich Von Schiller remarks:

There is no such thing as chance, and what seems to us merest accident springs from the deepest source of destiny.

Guru Amardas of the 15th/16th Centuries notes:

God himself forces his creatures into destined paths of karmas over which they have no control and which cannot be effaced. Whatever is destined to take place must take place.

Dr. Albert Einstein mirrors Guru Amardas's statement:

Everything is determined, the beginning as well as the end, by forces over which we have no control. It is determined for the insect, as well as for the star. Human beings, vegetables, or cosmic dust, we all dance to a mysterious tune, intoned in the distance by an invisible piper.

Notice the eerie similarity? Guru Amardas says, *over which they have no control* and Dr. Einstein says, *over which we have no control* – basically, the same phrase from a Saint and a scientist (separated by over four hundred years) except for the pronouns *they* and *we*. Stunning!

Saint Sawan Singh states: (*Spiritual Gems*, Letter #78)

The total number of breaths which one is to take till death, the morsels which one is to eat and the steps which one is to walk are all preordained at birth and no one can alter, decrease or increase them.

Saint Charan Singh weighs in: (*Quest for Light*, p.360)

All men come into this world with a destiny of their own which goes on pushing them relentlessly on the course already marked out for them.

And how is our destiny formed from life to life? It is our karmas, our actions from previous lives that determine what we will experience in this life. However, one solitary life cannot possibly reconcile all our karmas from previous lives. Thus, we remain trapped, imprisoned in the Wheel of Transmigration until all our karmas can be paid off.

So now we come back to power and its role in each of our lives and the destinies associated with those lives. The greater the degree of power we possess, the greater the karma, good or bad.

When we deeply understand this concept of power and karma, we would most likely rethink our desire and lust for power, position, status, fame, celebrity, notoriety. Everything gets magnified when power is present.

Dr. Samuel Johnson is recognized as one of the most distinguished writers and man of letters in all of literature. It was he who published *A Dictionary of the English Language* in 1755. Imagine such a task! In his famous poem, *The Vanity of Human Wishes*, he writes:

Unnumbered suppliants crowd Preferment's Gate, athirst for wealth and burning to be great; delusive fortune hears the incessant call; they mount, they shine, evaporate and fall!

Dr. Johnson's message echoes Thomas Gray's quote earlier in this chapter. Man is drawn to power and fortune. But the question needs to be asked, "What are the karmic manifestations of crowding *Preferment's Gate*, of gaining worldly fortune, especially power, which is often a by-product of fame and fortune.

The Roman Emperor Marcus Aurelius succinctly noted:

All is ephemeral—fame and the famous as well.

So if all is ephemeral, why do men sacrifice their future by seeking temporary power in this temporary life, especially when so much is at stake? Is, for example, 300,000,000 years of suffering worth the telling of one lie which harms others in this life? That's a bad, extremely bad, bargain.

Still, people lie or do untoward things daily, but those in power have much more to lose, obviously, because their decisions affect untold numbers of people. Truly, existing in a position of power is akin to walking on a dangerously slippery slope with incarcerating karmic consequences for innumerable lives. Therefore, doing the right and loving thing is the wise choice versus the selfish, self-serving negative choice.

Why do negative experiences happen to us? They happen because we humans have lost connection with the Divine. We have drifted so far away from our Spiritual Center that we have become internally deaf and blind to our supernal heritage, which has resulted in us being saturated with worldliness, carnality, materiality – all things external.

As Saint Kabir exclaims: (*Kabir, The Great Mystic*, p.102)

The world is blind, engulfed in utter darkness, but to whom can I explain this?

Swami Ji Maharaj corroborates Kabir's statement: (*With the Three Masters,* 5th edition, p.61)

This world is engulfed in the darkness of Ignorance.

Saint Jagat Singh pronounces:

There is nothing but utter darkness and misery in this world. It is, indeed, a place where the blind are leading the blind.

How perfectly accurate are these quotes about blindness? The irony is that we think we "see." The reality is, we don't.

Saint Namdev of the 13th Century said: (*Saint Namdev: His Life and Teachings,* J. R. Puri and V. K. Sethi, Radha Soami Satsang Beas, Punjab, India, 2nd edition, 1978, p.105)

What shall I do? The world sees and yet is blind. It has forsaken bliss and runs after earthly pursuits. It idolizes stones and slaughters divine beings.

Obviously, from the Saintly quotes above, all of us would do well to address our spiritual blindness and forsake our earthliness. It is our spiritual blindness and ignorance of Karmic Law that creates such havoc in our lives, havoc magnified by the degree of power we possess.

Abraham Lincoln, the 16th President of the United States, understood power. He noted:

Nearly all men can stand adversity, but if you want to test a man's character, give him power.

Suzanne Necker, 18th Century French writer, offered this astute observation common to all people who attain positions of power:

Fortune does not change men, it unmasks them.

Plato, the famous Greek philosopher, wisely said:

The measure of a man is what he does with power.

Given this knowledge, one has to wonder how any of us, especially those in a power position, would govern if we understood the karmic ramifications of our actions. Yet, we generally don't consider the karmic consequences of what we do, as is clearly evident in our daily behaviors and choices.

Even though this chapter has focused on the negative karma of power affecting our future lives, the positive manifestation of power is just as forceful but, obviously, directly opposite.

How glorious it would be for our future lives and the lives of others if we created loving, kind, caring, helpful, ethical, moral, honest, supportive, gracious, courageous, generous, disciplined, patient, peaceful, virtuous, tender, controlled, honorable, healthful and service-oriented actions all centered on the highest and best good of self and others?

Although this is not possible for the world's masses in general due to the spiritual design of this duality-based creation, it is possible for each of us to do, and we should do, not just because of the positive karma generated for our future life or lives, but simply because it's the right thing to do. Such positive actions are the fundamental basis of a spiritual way of life.

In brief summary, the Karma of Power is precarious because of the scope of the potential damage it generates. However, the good it can do is wonderful. We just have to be aware that what we do today will have serious karmic repercussions and ramifications for ourself, for others and for our future lives.

THE CAUTION OF POWER

Be ever careful of your power
in the hour of your glory.
Be ever careful of your arrogance
in the instance of your reign.
In a karmic world ever temporal,
your greatness is ephemeral,
and any abuses of your crown
will, unfailingly, circle back 'round
to you again!

Therefore, dear friend, take the highest road
but seek the lowest ground;
restrain the reins of your renown.
Be always humble, never proud;
do not, yourself, speak aloud
your fame or name or temporal power
as you rejoice within your tower.
Best let others shower you
with the rains of your acclaim.

All beg and pray for power and fame,
but few assess the heinous flames of same.
Their power blinds them.
Thus, they never heed

the dangers lurking in the Weeds of Rank,
and they forget as they go 'round,
*Uneasy lies the head that wears a crown.**
As light to dark and back again,
so circle fully acts of sin.

Thus, be cautious in your power
as you regale in your tower.
Note those below and shower them
with all the glory that's in Him,
for He and He alone is King,
and He and He alone will bring
to you His Blessèd Power
and save you from the Devil's Tower
as you go 'round and 'round again.

**Uneasy lies the head that wears a crown* – Shakespeare, Henry IV, Part 11, Act III, Scene 1

KINGDOMS AND KINGS

Kingdoms and kings, cultures and queens,
all rise and fall by Karmic Law.
Celebrities and nobodies,
Heroes and heroines,
Princes and paupers,
cheers and sneers,
the high and low
all bow before
the King
who rules
not by committee,
popularity or notoriety,
but by Divine Decree.

Uneasy truly lies the head that wears a crown,
and egos overblown will surely drown
under the weight of their
glorified presumption.
and consumption.

- So –

Let it be known that ultimately
what was reaped was sewn,
and that a self-appointed
and anointed crown
will only drown
the head of
him who
wears
it.

SEEDING AND REAPING

© Richard Andrew King

Be mindful of your seeding
for it will guarantee your reaping.
If you prefer no weeping
then be mindful of your seeding.

Your actions will be binding;
their reactions ever grinding
through sunshine, storms and lightning.
Therefore, keep on minding

Your every thought and action
and insignificant transaction.
There is no abstraction
to Karma's satisfaction.

We plant the seed, we reap the deed;
A message we must ever heed
If in our lives we have no need
to genuflect upon our knees . . . and bleed!

THE MONEY GOD

How vile is this moneyed world
where the great god, 'Money', rules;
where the evil money master
plays all to be his fools;
and his fools go rushing in
with greed and trickery as tools,
to cheat the unsuspecting –
for the slave of money drools,
drools to slurp and savor
the delights that money buys;
drools to feel green, cold, hard cash,
obtained from filthy lies –
wipe across hot drooling lips
and a salivating brow,
to sacrifice one's very soul
for satisfaction in the Now.
Woe be unto you, you fools,
for your money-loving sins,
to cheat and lie your way to wealth
for temporal satisfaction,
satisfaction which will bind you
to the hell where the Wheel turns,
where you, for countless ages,
will feel the fire as it burns.

No heart that's green with avarice,
will ever flee this world,
and runs the very real risk
of falling and being hurled
down into the green abyss
where mucous-laden drool,
drowns each money-loving slave
in a greed-drenched whirlpool.
Look around and see how money
magnetizes man.
The world chases money
in every continent and land.
Who is there who does not prostitute
his life to fill his purse?
Who is there who ever looks ahead
beyond the coming hearse?
Mammon is a mighty god,
and money's just one tool
he uses to entrap the soul
and color him the fool.
And fool he is, or she,
who serves this moneyed god,
for each of us will pay the price
for our actions as we trod
the landscape of this earthly land
and its treacherous terrain,
especially if we sacrificed

His Laws to quench our gain.
How short is life! How blind our greed!
How false our green intent;
but just as certain is His Hand
in dispensing punishment,
punishment for our moneyed sins,
for cheating others in their need,
for violating His Commands
and serving the demon, Greed.
One must be wise within this life
not to fall as prey
to the money-loving mammon god
who steers his prey away
from the chastity of action,
and the Conscience of the Pure,
from the need for satisfaction,
from the world and its allure.
There's more to life than money
and the pleasures that it buys,
but falling victim to its ploys,
means falling into skies
where turbulent pain and suffering
and a host of demons wait
to pounce upon the greedy soul
through the devil's dungeon gate;
and there it will receive
the fruit of all its deeds,

being forced to eat the filth
of its money-loving seeds;
and there will be no peace
within this green quagmire.
The punishment for avarice
is discipline by fire.

CHAPTER NINE

KARMA OF VICTIMHOOD

This is going to be a shock for many people, but the truth of this world is that no one is an innocent victim, no one, and, subsequently, there is no legitimate victimhood.

What's the drumbeat? Answer: we sow, we reap and we cannot reap what we do not sow, and what we are reaping now we ourselves have sewn before. Therefore, we are amiss if we think we're an innocent victim. We're not. Karmic Law rules this world, and if we feel we are a victim, we are greatly misinformed, ignorant and/or blind to the Divine Design of this world and how it functions, which is a grave disservice to us and the world at large.

Being a victim is one of the outstanding delusions of this world. We can't blame anyone for feeling like a victim because they may not understand the connection between this life and its actions and past lives and their actions. If we could see our past lives, we would absolutely know we're never a victim, but such vision only occurs as we climb higher on the Divine Ladder of Consciousness.

How often in real life do we ever blame ourselves for what seemingly happens to us from outside sources? Most likely never. However, what does happen to us may well be the karmic adjustment of our actions from a prior life.

In the overall picture of multiple lifetimes the drama may be totally different. As one scenario, let's say we go to a movie but arrive early and accidentally see the ending where a woman shoots a man dead for no apparent reason. We may think the woman is evil. But then we stay and watch the entire movie from the beginning and see that the woman was raped, her husband and children killed by the man she shot dead at the end of the movie. We now have a very different perspective, thus allowing our understanding to expand, revealing the karmic truth of the drama.

When we transfer this concept to our current life, what we see at any one time may not be the entire truth of what actually *is* because we have no knowledge of what *was* in a previous life that generated the drama in this life. Thus, we can never accurately judge what we see because what we see in current time is most probably only a portion of the greater drama whose genesis was in a past time.

True story. A young man was playing basketball with some of his buddies. In the course of the game, the left side of his face was severely injured, so much so that he had to have plastic surgery to repair the damage. As he was recuperating in his hospital bed, he was curious as to the karmic cause of the accident. He went into a meditative state and asked God to show him the reason for his injury.

Soon, an image appeared in his mind of an ancient time when he was with a band of marauding warriors pillaging a village. Swinging a mace (steel ball on a chain) in his right hand and reins in his left, he galloped through the village on a brown chestnut horse and struck a defenseless kneeling man, whose head was bowed no less, on the *left* side of his face, crushing it. At that point, the image stopped.

The man, therefore, had his answer given to him through this meditative process. To this day, the man can recount the experience perfectly, but he says that nothing changes. The image is always the same and stops at the very point in time when the mace he was swinging hit the defenseless man on the left side of his face, the same side of his own face that was injured while playing basketball. Coincidence? Maybe, but he swears it's the truth.

During this entire event of having his face damaged, going through plastic surgery and being hospitalized, the man never considered himself a victim. However, understanding karma, he was curious as to the sowing of the reaping he had just experienced. Going into meditation and asking for an explanation gave him his answer, which was that in his past he damaged the left side of another man's face and so in this life the left side of his own face was damaged. Perfect justice, not an eye for an eye but definitely a damaged face for a damaged face. Basically, he reaped exactly what he had sewn. Karma paid; case closed.

Not seeing ourselves as a victim when we are injured, or beset with some challenging situation, is often difficult because Karmic Law and reincarnation are not considered basic principles of life for most of humanity. Yet, Saints inform us that reincarnation and karma are integral aspects of this world's spiritual architecture. Therefore, we can either accept this reality and work with it or ignore it and attempt to live in denial, which will not help us grow spiritually or remain balanced and centered.

Some people may believe that if they perform actions in secret they will escape the consequences. Not so. Saint Sawan Singh states: (*Philosophy of the Masters*, Vol. 1, p.22)

One cannot escape the result of one's actions by performing them in secret. The consequences of such actions have to be borne sometime or the other. It is therefore clear that whatever weal or woe, joy or sorrow we experience, it is all due to our own actions, and we should not blame anyone else for it.

IT'S GOD'S FAULT

When accidents or tragedies happen in people's lives, a familiar refrain is, "It's God's fault." Without a deeper knowledge of how this world and creation function, it is understandable that people would blame God, since some accidents and tragedies offer no common explanation otherwise. It is natural that people may think this. However, God is not responsible for the accidents and tragedies in our lives. We are, and the reason rests in Karmic Law.

Saints teach that when this world was created, there had to be souls to inhabit it. That would be us. When we made our first action in this world, a natural reaction was generated according to the Karmic Algorithm. After the first reaction, we made another action which generated yet another reaction, and so the karmic process began and continued unabated as the primary Law of this world. Millions of years later, and after migrating through millions of living forms in the Wheel of Transmigration, we have arrived in this life as human beings. Lucky us.

Now, during our existence in other forms of life, such as plants, insects, fish, birds and animals, we have done a lot of things, some good, some bad. Among the bad, have been countless killings of other creatures for multiple reasons. We don't remember any of these lives in other forms because the memory of our past is erased after each life.

When we did these killings, those whom we killed became our victims. They all had a mother and a father, perhaps even siblings. We gave no thought at all to their suffering. These killings demanded, by Karmic Law, that we be killed in return, that we become a victim – of our own making. After all, every action has its equal and opposite reaction, i.e., karma. We create victims; we become the victim.

But killing other living beings is not the only way we have victimized ourselves. How many times in how many lives in how many ways have we lied, cheated, deceived, thieved, obstructed, denied, vilified, falsified, slandered, betrayed, hurt, destroyed, damaged, maligned, maimed or in any way injured or caused harm to another living being, either socially, physically, psychologically, emotionally, financially, familially?

In contrast, how much time have we spent thinking of how our actions have had a negative effect and impact on others? Probably not too much. Yet, all of these actions we have perpetrated on others have returned to us and will continue to return to us via Karmic Law. Our natural reaction, sans enlightenment, will be to blame others and play the victim card. Yet, do we really have the right to do so? Are we really an innocent victim in anything? Karma says, "No. We sowed, we reaped, we weeped, we became a victim by our own doing, not someone else's."

This brings us to the point of recompense – the karmic time to pay up. Accidents, tragedies, hardships, etc., are nothing more than Karmic Law in action – the repaying of karmic debts from previous lives now seeking retribution.

Thus, it's not God's fault for what we experience in life; it's our fault. We must remember, God doesn't prevent us from making choices; nor does He prevent us from experiencing the consequences of those choices. When we kill, we must be killed – sooner or later. When we play the part of the killer, we eventually must play the part of the victim, and when we are the victim, it is no one else's fault but our own. The same thing goes for all the untoward things we've done in the past. We could not be the victim unless we had created victims through our own negative and nefarious actions.

But Mary Jane Doe asks, "What of innocent little children who have been victimized by some means?" Karmic Law would retort, "How many of those "innocent little children," whom you call victims, killed, hurt, maimed or injured or in any way harmed innocent children in their previous lives?"

It is tragic that little children or any children become victims in this life, but the reality is that we sow, we reap and we cannot reap what we do not sow. When we victimize others, we will eventually become victimized. None of us in this world does not have blood on our hands for all the killing and harm we have done in previous lives. None of us, none, is a victim unless it is a victim by our own doing.

The good news is that we now have a human body – the Crown Jewel of creation – and we can change the course of our life and future lives by making more spiritual choices. Living by a vegetarian diet in order to put an end to this egregious Killer/Victim Cycle of our own creation is one of the wisest and most salient of the choices we have the opportunity to make now so that we can move upward on the Ladder of Consciousness and eventually exit this nether world. In fact, exiting this world is why Saints have been sent here, i.e., to help us escape. As Saint Charan Singh has stated many times in many ways:

You do not belong to this world. Just live
in the world and get out of it!

And from *The King's Book of Numerology, Volume 1 – Foundations & Fundamentals*, page 73, we read:

Perfect Master Maharaj Charan Singh Ji says, "There are no innocent victims" in this dimension. We all reap exactly what we have sown and there is no escaping this fact. It is Law in this creation. If we plant seeds of fire, we will reap seeds of fire. If we plant seeds of sorrow, we will reap seeds of sorrow. Likewise, if we plant seeds of love, harmony, purity, balance, generosity, honesty, honor and right behavior, we will reap their fruit. In essence, we generate the vehicles of our own purification. We are the sculptors of our own destiny, our own pain, our own suffering, our own cleansing.

TEACHING CHILDREN

Seeing ourselves as a victim is not an honest point of view and diminishes us as independent, sovereign, strong, capable, courageous, valorous, determined, intrepid, resilient, wise, whole, imperturbable, enlightened, secure and sentient human beings.

When we teach our children either by example or directive to play the part of the victim, we deny them the critical opportunity of growing into everything and more that the previous paragraph illuminates. In such denial we weaken them, cripple them and make them less whole. In effect, we do a grave disservice to them.

Rather, we would do well to teach our children to never play the victim but portray the hero or heroine instead. Reveling as a victim screams weakness and helplessness. It does not serve our children well. Plus, it continues the false narrative of victimhood while negating the truth of karmahood. The sooner our children understand this truth the better they and their lives will be for it.

In summary, this chapter has focused on one main reality, which is that we are never an innocent victim; that we become a victim through our own actions of making other people our victims, thus guaranteeing our becoming a victim by Karmic Law.

Indeed, this is a difficult truth to accept, but if we want to climb the Spiritual Ladder, we have no other choice but to work within the Law and not do our best to deny it. By denying it, we only strengthen the delusion of victimhood. By living within the Law, we not only help ourselves but we help everyone else in our own personal worlds, whether by being a living example of what it's like to not play the victim or through verbal instruction. Either way, we win, as does everyone else around us.

Saints understand victimhood more than anyone else. Do they ever blame someone or something else for their actions? Absolutely not. We leave this chapter with several quotes: one from Guru Nanak and two from Saint Charan Singh. Guru Nanak states: (*Guru Nanak*, p.203)

I blame not another. I blame my own karmas.
Whatever I sowed, so did I reap. Why then
put the blame on others?

Saint Charan Singh echoes the same principle: (*Quest for Light*, Letter #231)

> *Our present life is the result of our own actions*
> *in the past and we cannot blame anyone for it.*

And: (*Quest for Light*, Letter #233)

The Creator never rewards or punishes one without a cause. 'As you sow, so shall you reap' is the unalterable law of this universe and no one can change it. In the face of this law, who is to blame?

The take away is that this life and every life is our responsibility, not someone else's. Through our own actions, we are the architects of our fate. As much as we may like to play the victim, we cannot. We can try, of course, but such is a fool's gambit. The Karmic Drumbeat continues to roll – what we sow, we reap, and we cannot reap what we do not sow.

ARCHITECTS

We are the architects of our fate
through seeds of lifetimes sown.
Every aspect of our fate
is by our own hand grown.

All our pains and sufferings,
and failures soon or late,
come encircling back to us –
the architects of our fate.

Deeds are seeds; their fruit our loot,
whether wicked, good or great.
There is no mistaking –
we are the architects of our fate.

Lament in tears or smile in glee,
excoriate or congratulate.
Nothing can repudiate –
that we are the architects of our fate.

How soon we understand this Law –
that our fate's by our hand sown –
determines our Ascension
into the Great Unknown

where we will live Forever,
having entered through His Gate,
realizing His Great Law –
that we are the architects of our fate.

Richard Andrew King

WE ARE NO VICTIM

© Richard Andrew King

We are no victim, no matter what we say;
we sow, we reap. Such is the Karmic Way.
Whatever dramas our life portrays,
it is Karmic Law that rules our days.
No one is an innocent victim here
in this nether world of joy and fear.
No one can claim to be a victim
in a world ruled by Karmic Dictum.
Every action that we make
generates reaction in its wake;
we cannot reap what we do not sow;
for killing others, we reap woe.
Yet, for every action that is good,
we reap rewards, as well we should,
but when we cultivate evil seeds,
we reap the evil of our deeds.
Truly, we're no victim in this Netherland;
we function by the Lord's command;
we reap what Karmic Law demands
from planting seeds with our own hands.

VICTIMHOOD and KARMAHOOD

From babyhood to manhood,
childhood to adulthood;
in truth there is no Victimhood
within this Karmahood.

"I blame all others," cries Victimhood.
"I blame no others," cries Karmahood.
We sow, we reap, as well we should.
It is the Law in this Neighborhood.

Within the milieu of its falsehood
the world lives in Victimhood;
when cause and consequence are understood,
one gains maturity in Karmahood.

~ for now ~

Delusion thrives in Victimhood,
the suburbs of this Devilwood.
Yet, in ascent to Heavenwood,
we don the robes of Saintlyhood,

~ and then ~

we rise above this Netherwood
and say goodbye to Victimhood,
surpassing even Karmahood
and dwelling in Enlightenhood.

Richard Andrew King

NETHERLAND

This is the land of the Negative Power
where only darkness rules.
This is the land made great with death
where there are no virtue schools.
This is the place duplicity reigns,
the snare of 'woman- man';
This is the Dungeon of Darkness.
This is Netherland.

-so-

Enter ye who choose to be
captives of the night;
once within, escape is dim,
and all that is, is fright.

When we step in
this labyrinth den,
anguish fills the air;
moaning, groaning, wailing cries
make it hard to bear;
deceiving, scheming, lying tongues
steal what we own,
and the gravity of the depravity
erases thoughts of Home.

-so-

Enter ye who choose to be
captives of the night;
once within, escape is dim,
and all that is, is fright.

This Devil's lair is fashioned fair
to trap us with delights;
to magnetize our wayward eyes
with streams of wonders bright.
Yet, his Net is intricate;
few escape its thread;
peace is non-existent
with nightmares in the bed.

-so-

Enter ye who choose to be
captives of the night;
once within, escape is dim,
and all that is, is fright.
Killing is the way of all
who live within this realm.
It can't be any other way
with the Devil at the helm.
He has no other purpose
than to rule by wicked sin,
and only those who do succeed
live to worship him.

-so-

Enter ye who choose to be
captives of the night;
once within, escape is dim,
and all that is, is fright.

The greatest of delusions
as we dwell within this den,
is to think that when we die
we, somehow, go to Heaven.
How slick, how sick
this Devil does deceive,
to offer us this can of trash
and this bag of wind believe.

-so-

Enter ye who choose to be
captives of the night;
once within, escape is dim,
and all that is, is fright.

The alarming ken within this den
is the Wheel of Eighty-Four –
eight million, four hundred thousand forms,
each with a private door;
each with a different body,
each with a different cell,

each with a different outlook
of its private life in hell.

-so-

Enter ye who choose to be
captives of the night;
once within, escape is dim;
and all that is, is fright.

The great, sad fact of all this talk
is that we're already in,
living in the Darkness,
of the Devil's Dungeon Den;
suffering on the Wheel,
boiling in indigent plight,
and the only way to save the day
is to call His Name by night.

If we do seek His Presence,
if we live by His might,
if we adjust our erring ways
to manifest His Light,
if we disclaim all loyalty
to the Devil's ruling hand,
then there is hope that God Supreme
will save us from Netherland.

But if we don't, then 'cest la vie';
Netherland will be home
for another million ages;
another million lives alone,
and we'll remain in darkness,
wailing in the night,
praying, still, with all our will
for Him to end our plight.

-so-

Seek the Lord, the One Supreme,
and rise into His Sky;
Enter In the Great Within
where you can never die;
dedicate your every breath
to recitation of His Name,
and you will exit Netherland
and win life's greatest Game,

and know, in fact, that Netherland
is the Devil's world,
and if you don't escape his claws,
once more you will be hurled
back into the labyrinth
where the hope of life is lost
for millions upon millions

of lives – such is the dreaded cost.
But time *is* running out;
numbered are our breaths;
if we don't make Connection
with the Lord we'll never rest.
Our true and only lifeline
is the Current* and its Light;
if we don't carve our place in it
we *will* be cast into the night

Of a deep, foreboding Wheel
where's the soul's forever tossed
from form to form in agony;
where the truth of God is lost;
where the hope of our Salvation
and the Liberation of our soul
will never be an issue,
for the mind will never know

Within the Wheel's depths
that there is a God,
that there is eternity
for those who seek to trod
the Path of Sound and Light
that is truly liberating,
a Path of Holy Energy
and a Current* captivating.

Awake, Dear Soul! Do not neglect
to heed this warning true;
the human form is for Escape,
that's why it's gifted you;
Your time is running out
as you breathe your every breath;
if you don't act now while alive,
you'll live regret in death.

Hell is real. So is the Wheel.
Human life's not ours to choose.
If we don't use it while we can,
Tragically, regretfully, we lose.

So enter ye who choose to be
Disciples of the Right;
once Within, our slavery ends,
and all there is, is Light!

Do not delay; do not avoid;
heed this warning true:
Kabir, the Mystic, utters clear,
Remain not unconcerned. I warn you!

*Current – a reference to the Sound Current or Word of God taught by Saints. See *Messages of the Masters – Timeless Truths for Spiritual Seekers* by Richard Andrew King

Richard Andrew King

CHAPTER TEN

KARMA OF LOVE

Nothing in this world is more powerful, sublime, uplifting, comforting and healing than love. Its vibration transcends every other quality of life in this dimension.

We all know how we feel when we're loved – warm, safe, secure, ecstatic. Is there any feeling or emotion that is better? What living being does not respond positively when loved? Therefore, when we love we give the greatest gift of all and cast invisible waves of peace, joy, happiness, comfort and bliss throughout the lives of those we touch, even beyond. There is no greater karma than giving and receiving the karma of love.

How can we define love? In its most elevated definition, God is love and love is God. But God is infinite. Therefore, love must be infinite and beyond definition.

Generally, love is defined as affection or sexual attraction. However, spiritual love transcends the worldly definition of love as sexuality, the latter being more a condition of lust than love.

In *The Master Answers* we read the following: (p.145)

The difference in spiritual love and worldly love is this: In spiritual love you are not conscious of anybody except the object of your love, except your Master or the Lord. In worldly love you are always conscious of others; there is instinct of possession, and then jealousy comes in when you are conscious of others. In spiritual love, there can be no jealousy, for you have forgotten the whole world; whether it exists for you or not, you are just in Him. That is the difference.

Saint Charan Singh further explains the difference between love and lust in *Divine Light*. The word "Kal" is a reference to the Negative Power, i.e., Satan. (Radha Soami Satsang Beas, 4th edition, 1976, p.313)

Do not call lust by the name of Love. There is a vast difference between Love and lust. God and Love are the same. Love lifts up. Lust pulls us down. Love is light. Lust is heavy. In lust there is suffering and grief, but in Love there is unity and joy. Love is the expression of the Soul. Lust is the craving of the senses. In Love there is tranquility. In lust there is excitement. Love is the gift of the Lord. Lust is an instrument of Kal. Love leads to freedom. Lust leads to complications. Love is Godly. Lust is hellish.

True love, supernal love, is not temporary. It is eternal and timeless. Says Saint Charan Singh: (*Legacy of Love*, private memoriam, p.29)

Love means that which lasts forever. It doesn't diminish. It always grows and grows and grows and grows. If love comes, it never goes. If it goes, it is not love.

Unlike worldly relationships, which are based in selfish motives, the accrual of advantage and usefulness, true love, spiritual love, is just the opposite. The following six words from Saint Charan Singh are even more profound than they are succinct:

Love never calculates; it just gives.

In other words, when we truly love we never consider the benefits and advantages that will accrue to us in the process of loving. Selfish desires never enter our mind, let alone our heart. When we love purely, we just give and give with no expectation of getting anything in return.

From *The Master Answers* we read: (p.143)

The more you give love, the more it grows. The more you share it, the more you will have it in abundance.

From a karmic perspective, therefore, we can know how much we have loved in the past based on how much love we are experiencing in the present. If our life is not reflective of much love, it means we have not loved purely enough, obviously because we have not sewn the threads of love into the fabric of our life. If we haven't sewn love, how can we reap love?

However, if our lives are filled with love, it is because we have sewn loving seeds in our prior lives and their blooming is our current reaping. We are the architects of our fate and we're living that fate every second of every day. In every way, our present life experiences are a manifestation of our past actions due to Karmic Law.

It is common for people to tell someone they love, "I love you." Yet, saying "I love you," is meaningless unless our actions support our words. In fact, if we truly love, we don't even need to use words at all. Our actions will reflect the honesty of our love. Frankly, unannounced love is more powerful than spoken love because actions speak louder than words. Which type of love would you rather have – words with no connection to reality or simply the reality sans words? We all know the answer.

In fact, Saint Charan Singh declares: (Ibid., p.468)

Love has no language.

And of course this is a true statement, isn't it? How freely our emotions flow, often in tears, when we witness a genuine act of love, such as someone being saved from mayhem or death by a selfless and unknown person rushing to save the individual without any regard for their own safety? Or a pet lovingly lying beside its owner, especially when the human is ill, to protect him/her? Or a little child offering comfort to another little child? Or an athlete interrupting their event to help another athlete in trouble? We've all witnessed such heroic acts of love and kindness. They're universal, and they're not based in words. They're based in selfless loving action.

The obvious rub for most of us, if not all of us, is that supernal love is what we're working toward and learning to develop, that is if we're spiritually focused. It takes time to evolve into loving purely, honestly, genuinely. If we're worldly minded, we're most likely existing in the "what can I get out of this loving situation?" mindset. If we're spiritually minded, we just love without expectation. We simply give.

However, our love should not be restricted to humans. Remember the following quote from Saint Charan Singh related to living by a vegetarian diet? Notice the emphasis on love. (*The Master Answers*, p.298)

(Vegetarian diet) *We must follow it. There is no other way for spiritual progress . . . If we kill, we will be killed. We should never forget that. Christ said, "Love thy neighbor." All creatures are our neighbors . . . When you love anybody, you do not kill that individual; and when we love the whole creation, we cannot kill intentionally, nor could we find it in our heart to have it done for us by someone else.*

So in expanding our consciousness of love, perhaps one way to get started is to change to a vegetarian diet. Not only does it keep us from adding to our negative karmic load but it also assists us in learning to love all living beings, not just humans.

The value of true love is not restricted to diet. As Saint Sawan Singh comments: (*The Dawn of Light*, p.65)

Wherever there is love, there is life. Where there is no love, life is worthless.

This sentiment is expanded by Saint Kabir: (*Kabir*, p.365)

Where there is Love, there is no law, there is no logic and no reasoning. You do not care if it is an auspicious or an inauspicious day, or even whether it is day or whether it is night when you are deeply intoxicated with the Love Divine.

Love is not only universal, it is the commandment to all of us. As Christ states: (*Bible*, KJV, John 13:34)

A new commandment I give unto you, That ye love one another as I have loved you; that ye also love one another.

Saint Dariya of Bihar says: (*Dariya Sahib – Saint of Bihar*, K.N. Upadhyaya, Radha Soami Satsang Beas, Punjab, India, 1987, p.303)

Without love there is no spiritual path. The path lives in love.

However, Dariya also makes it clear that the Path is not easy to follow. Very directly he declares: (Ibid., p.81)

The path of love is very steep.

Kabir cautions: (*Kabir*, p.364)

Thy mystic path is the path of Love supreme; but following it is no cheap or easy task.

The greatest accomplishments in life are never easy. In fact, they're quite difficult. Living in the spirit and action of love is, arguably, the greatest of the great when it comes to human behavior. So if we want to expand our love quotient, where do we begin, especially if we feel unloved? Says Saint Sawan Singh: (*Spiritual Gems*, Letter #178)

The best way to get the love of others is first to give great love to others.

Saint Dadu teaches: (*Dadu*; p.141)

Develop love and devotion with endearment and keep the thought of the Creator always before thee.

In this process of developing love, we will be wise to remember this quote from Saint Charan Singh: (*The Master Answers*; p.385)

A heart full of love has no room for hatred.

And a warning: (Ibid., 279)

When we hate anybody, actually we are hating ourselves.

How often do we think of this – that our hatred of others is really a hatred of us? This is excellent food for thought. And it is true because we can't hate if there is no hate in us. We only hate when there is hate in us.

Likewise, we can only love when there is love in us, and we cannot love if there is no love within us. Living love, experiencing love, does not begin with others loving us, it begins with us and our expression of love. The planting always precedes the harvesting. Therefore, we have no right to feel negatively if we neither feel love nor experience love. If we want love, we must create it and place it onto the circle of life. By Karmic Law it will then naturally circle back to encircle us eventually.

Summarily, it is no easy thing to master the true art of loving. It is a selfless quality demanding constant vigilance, sacrifice and an unrelenting focus on building a consciousness of love. As we reap what we sow, we also live in the architectural structure of our own design and making.

As we continue on this journey of everlasting life, what kind of future life do we want to build? What kind of karmas do we want to experience? What kind of legacy do we want to leave behind? One of love? Let us hope so.

The reality, however, is that everything - positive or negative, good or bad - begins with us, with our own actions. Love begins from the inside and flows outwardly. We sow, we reap and we cannot reap what we do not sow. Where have we heard this before? Therefore, let us live in love and do all that we can to share its vibration with others.

LOVE

As man extends his wandering palm
across a universe of space,
and catapults his mind
into distant realms of infinity;
as he seeks the planes of the great unknown,
and strives to soar within
the corridors of the free;
as he struggles up the stairway
of his consciousness,
forever gaining sight of mastery,
repelling thoughts of imperfection,
denying captive limitation;
as he fights to win,
to be heralded
as the conqueror of his life,
then, surely,
must he come to know,
that Love is the manifestation
and the Light of the Living Soul.

CHAPTER ELEVEN

KARMA OF SUICIDE AND SLANDER

There are two subjects that especially need to be addressed because their karmic ramifications are critical to note and understand. These two subjects are suicide and slander.

Suicide is the action of a person taking his/her own life. Spiritually, this is very dangerous because although we think our life belongs to us, it does not. The human body is a divine gift given to us to rise higher on the Spiritual Ladder, eventually gaining our release from this nether world. By committing suicide we disclaim the gift.

In *Quest for Light* Saint Charan Singh discusses suicide at great length, repeating the message multiple times to drive the point home that suicide is a great sin encompassing severe consequences. He says:

All our karmas (the results of our thoughts and actions) go with us to the next life with an added sin of suicide if we succumb to such an act. We can never escape from reaping what we have sown by cutting short our life. On the contrary, we would only make our burden still heavier. (Letter #145)

In Letter #328 of *Quest for Light* Saint Charan Singh addresses the act of suicide further in direct response to a letter from an individual who actually attempted suicide. Very clearly and directly, he states:

I am surprised to read that you even tried to take your own life. There is no greater sin than that. Do you in any way escape from your karmas when you do that? All the uncleared karmas go with you to the next life with the additional very heavy load of suicide. The next life will be much more miserable with this additional load of unforgivable sin. Never think, not even in your dreams, to take your own life.

He further emphasizes the point in Letter #415: (Ibid.)

No Master will ever advise anyone to commit suicide... Suicide is a heinous sin and a very heavy penalty has to be paid for taking one's life... Never think, not even in dreams, of such a thing as suicide.

From letter #432: (Ibid.)

Suicide is a heinous sin and is unpardonable. The gates of hell are wide open for one who commits suicide. We have no right to take our own or anyone else's life. This life is a rare privilege and we have to go through our destiny bravely and courageously. . . No Master has ever advised nor will He ever advise anyone to commit suicide or to take anyone else's life.

Also from Letter #432 we read: (Ibid.)

By committing suicide we do not escape from our karmas, but carry them to the next life with the additional very heavy sin of suicide. Please bear in mind that nothing can justify this act of madness and it should never be in your thoughts. No such thought should ever enter anyone's mind, not even in dreams. It is a terrible sin and means a very heavy burden followed by correspondingly heavy punishment.

And more from Letter #459: (Ibid.)

Suicide is a very great sin and entails an extremely heavy burden. It should never be thought of by anyone. A person commits suicide in order to escape from his present suffering, but does not realize that the karma he is paying off through this suffering will have to be paid in the next life with the additional burden and sin of suicide. One can never escape from reaping what one has sown. Karmic accounts have to be cleared, if not in this life, then in another one. Karmas are never forgotten, ignored or overlooked. They have to be paid.

After this lengthy set of quotes, can anyone doubt that suicide is a great sin whose karmas are devastating and incarcerating? Therefore, whatever karmas we are challenged with in this life, it is better to endure them now rather than trying to avoid them, which is impossible. Taking our own life only compounds the karmic debt with which we are already strapped.

Obviously, we do not make our life easier by attempting to escape our troubles via the act of suicide. We must never, as Saint Charan Singh states multiple times, even think of suicide in our dreams.

Whatever our karma is now, we have to deal with it now, not try to run away from it or negate it through suicide. Our life will only get worse, much worse, if we take our own life. Death, by any means, is not the end of life, although it may be the end of this incarnation. We must live it and deal with its karmas but never try in any way to escape it because we won't be able to do so.

As this work has stated multiple times, human life is the Top of Creation, the Crown Jewel of all living species, a precious gift given to us after millions of lives. If we dishonor our life via the madness of suicide, what can we honestly expect? A better life next time? No. This will never happen; just the reverse, even worse. Chapter Seven discussed the dangers of abortion of a fetus. Suicide is an abortion of our own life and just as heinous an act of killing, guaranteeing us a dark and foreboding future.

All this being said, therefore, we need to understand the depth of the problem and solve it now while we're in this body, in this life. If we're suicidal or know someone who is, we need to get help or offer help to them. Activating the suicide button, be it the trigger of a gun, a hangman's noose, a needle in the arm, a jump off a cliff or out a window, whatever, is a ticket to hell and a more hellish future. Nothing good will come of an act of suicide, nothing. Quite to the contrary. But when we fight our suicidal demons through courage, strength, humility, faith, determination, prayer and win, as win we must, we'll be able to move on and upward to a more advantageous life.

SLANDER

Slander is the unjustifiable defamation of someone, their good name or reputation by misrepresentation, malicious or false charges. When someone slanders another person, the slanderer (the one doing the slandering) is attempting to injure the slanderee (the one being slandered) by speaking ill of that person.

When slanderous comments are put in writing, the result is called libel and the slanderer is being libelous. Either way, the goal is to defame, injure or hurt someone unjustifiably.

There are ponderous spiritual consequences for the slanderer, which are little known to the masses but, nonetheless, highly detrimental, consequences which any sane person would not want to experience. When this knowledge is known, people who indulge in slanderous behavior would be well-served to pay attention to the nefarious wagging of their tongue.

The following Saintly quotes reveal why slandering others is not just unwise but highly disadvantageous for the slanderer. We'll label this knowledge as the Slander Law.

Saint Sawan Singh states: (*With the Three Masters*; Vol I, p.186)

When people who speak ill of others touch gold it turns to dust, said the Master, and all the bad karmas of persons spoken ill of are transferred to them and their own good karmas are transferred to the former.

Let's clarify this a little. Imagine that we all have a karmic bank account of good and bad karmas. When we slander someone, all of our good karmas are automatically transferred to the account of the person we slander. In other words, money is taken out of our account, depleting it of our karmic savings, and given to the slanderee.

But it gets worse. Not only are our good karmas given to people we slander, but their bad karmas, their debts, are automatically transferred to our account! Thus, we lose in two ways: 1. we lose our karmic savings and 2. we acquire the debts of the soul we slandered. How unwise is this? And why does this happen? It happens because we engage in speaking ill of others; in trying to defame them, hurt them, injure them. Woe be unto us if we engage in slanderous activity! Such is the purity of Karmic Justice!

In *The Science of the Soul,* Saint Jagat Singh corroborates the Slander Law: (p.206)

All the good deeds of one who talks ill of another are credited to the account of the slandered one. The slanderer washes away our sins without charging us anything.

Saint Kabir states: (*Kabir, The Great Mystic*; p.408)

Welcome the slanderer, for the slanderer is a blessing. He brings cool shade to thy poor grass-thatched hut and to thy kitchen garden also. He washes thee quite clean without any water or soap and makes thee pure as the mountain's whitest snow.

Kabir even shares this idea in poetic form: (Ibid., p.279)

Send not thy slanderer away; give him all respect and honor; For he talks nonsense, and washes clean thy body and mind.

And a similar quote:

O Lord, let not my slanderer die; may he live for ever and ever; for through his cleansing grace, I reached the feet of my Master.

Understanding this Slander Law and its disastrous effects on the slanderer, why would any sentient individual ever slander anyone?

Slandering people is a two-edged sword. We lose good karma and are forced to take on bad karma. We throw away our karma credit and acquire unwanted, but not undeserved or unjustified, debt. Obviously, we should not only be careful what we wish for in life, but we should also be extremely careful of engaging in slander.

In summary of our engaging in suicide or slander, one sound, spiritual, critical piece of advice is to avoid them at all costs. Suicide sends us to hell. Slander sends us to the poor house. Nothing good will result from these two heinous acts of utter nonsense.

SUICIDE

It is the greatest crime against the Lord.
For it, hell-gates open wide.
It spits upon His very Face,
this act of suicide.

To take our life glares Disrespect.
This body – we don't own.
He freely gives it to us
so we can journey Home.

So when we deprecate it
by killing it for show,
He takes offense and sends us
to the lowest hell below.

There we stay and there we pay,
and there we yearn and burn,
until He feels our punishment
is satisfactory to return

us once again to higher ground,
where we can run His race;
where we can learn to honor Him,
and not spit upon His Grace.

Richard Andrew King

THE SLANDER RULE

© Richard Andrew King

Oh! How we slander and play the fool
by spewing lies with caustic drool;
all designed to damage and defame
another from his life's good name.

Within our zeal to play the mule
we fill our tanks with endless fuel
of all that's dark and filled with lies
to satisfy our ghoulish eyes.

But while we smirk with ridicule,
we fail to see the Karmic Rule,
where we will forfeit all our gain,
and gain more debts unto our name!

In payment for our being cruel
we're anchored to the Dunce's Stool;
so ignorant and unwise are we
to slander others in evil glee!

CHAPTER TWELVE

KARMA AND NUMEROLOGY

Numerology is the science of numeric coding defining and describing our lives, relationships and destinies via our full birth name and birth date. It can also be defined as the numeric manifestation of the architectural design of life and destiny.

Although numerology is considered New Age, nothing could be further from the truth. Numbers were before man was. Moreover, numbers are the most universal communication system known to intelligent life. What is there that cannot be reduced to numbers, numerical patterns or numerical structures? Numerology will come alive when people see how their lives are reflected in their numbers and then a New Age will dawn for them.

Richard Andrew King

As famed mathematician Pythagoras (of the Pythagorean Theorem) stated over 2500 years ago:

Numbers rule the universe. Everything is arranged according to number and mathematical shape.

Light, sound, music, computers and destiny can all be reduced to numbers. Even our karmas are revealed in numbers. Why is this? It is because numbers, other than being arithmetic ciphers, are God codes, labels for energy fields. Just as gravity is an invisible force, so numbers are identifying markers for the invisible forces of our lives and destinies. Numbers are a language unto themselves and when we understand the language of numeric coding, we gain access to a wealth of knowledge and a consciousness of reality we never new existed.

Isaac Newton, arguably the greatest scientist who ever lived, declared:

God created everything by number, weight and measure.

Here we see the reality of numbers again. These great minds (Pythagoras and Newton) are great for a reason – they have moved beyond the realm of ordinary thought into the region of thinking beyond the norm, beyond the mundane, beyond the myopic mindset of common perception.

Additionally, numbers and letters (which have numerical equivalents) form the basis of our destiny, and as strange as it may seem, the blueprint of that destiny for each of us is contained within our full name at birth and our birth date. And perhaps even stranger is that our karmas are, to some degree, manifested in our numbers. It is amazing, but true.

This concept is easy to understand when we see ourselves as energy, not just as a human body, which has been discussed before. Our energy never dies. It moves from life to life, form to form. Our karmas are the energetic manifestation of our actions and reactions, and because they, too, are energy they never die either but go with "us" wherever we go within the Wheel of Transmigration.

When we're born as humans, the date of birth and our birth name are generated from the structure of the karmic energies of our past lives. Numbers are the labels for those energies. They are not happenstance but the structural components used to craft our destinies by higher powers.

Strange? Weird? Unbelievable? Crazy? We may think so, but when we study the relationship between our numbers and our lives on a day to day basis, we see a reality of life that is stunning and perfect. Each of our lives is not an accident. It is the result of a divine design generated by a Power far beyond our meager ability to comprehend but, nonetheless, we can see this divine design in operation via the numbers and number patterns of our life's blueprint as expressed through our own numerology chart.

Exactly why our karmas are the way they are in this life is impossible to fully know because we have created so many karmas in previous lives. There's not just a little bit of karma from our past. There are mountain ranges of it. The Power that generates our destiny in this life draws karmic energy from the massive storehouse of karmas of our previous lives and designs our destiny based on those karmas, which are identified by the numeric components of our birth name and birth date.

For those individuals who don't believe in destiny, the following quotes are offered for consideration.

Everything is determined, the beginning as well as the end, by forces over which we have no control. It is determined for the insect, as well as for the star. Human beings, vegetables or cosmic dust – we all dance to a mysterious tune, intoned in the distance by an invisible piper.

~ Dr. Albert Einstein

God himself forces his creatures into destined paths of karmas (fruits of previous actions) over which they have no control and which cannot be effaced. Whatever is destined to take place must take place.

~ Guru Amardas

Please do not forget that all men come into this world with a destiny of their own which goes on pushing them relentlessly on the course already marked out for them. Man is completely helpless. Then why worry? . . . Nothing can happen which is not in your destiny.

~ Saint Charan Singh

Before a person is born, his entire life or destiny is settled . . . Whatever is happening is all preordained . . . We are powerless to change our destiny. Whatever is destined in our fate must happen . . . The law of karma (results of past actions) and the doctrine of predestination and preordination are true and inexorable. We reap what we sow! Our actions in past lives bring about our "fate" in this life on which our bodies are fashioned . . . The total number of breaths which one is to take till death, the morsels which one is to eat and the steps which one is to walk are all preordained at birth and no one can alter, decrease or increase them.

~ Saint Sawan Singh

But even the hairs of your head are all numbered.

~ Bible, Matthew 10:30

There is no such thing as chance, and what seems to us merest accident springs from the deepest source of destiny.

~ Johann Friedrich Von Schiller

No living man can send me to the shades before my time; no man of woman born, coward or brave, can shun his destiny.

~ Homer

This list of quotes could be much longer but it drives the point home that, indeed, we all have a destiny, a fated existence.

The numeric reality is that we do not have a certain destiny because we were born with a certain name on a certain date, but rather we were born with a certain name on a certain date *because* we have a certain destiny based on our karmas of past lives. In other words, the destiny created the name and birthdate; the name and birthdate did not create the destiny, although the name and birthdate house the framework of the destiny.

There are many numbers and numeric components to a numerology chart. Every number or number pattern represents certain attributes and characteristics. By understanding the language of numbers and their placement in a chart we can decipher the blueprint of our destiny, as well as why we are the way we are, what our major lessons in life are, what we desire, need and want; where we're going, when we'll get there, what hurdles and challenges do we have to overcome, what our assets and liabilities are, when major changes will occur in our lives and so much more.

The thing is that every number in our chart is there for a karmic reason, and we're responsible for each of those numbers being there based on our actions from the past, actions which, energetically, manifest in the present as numbers in our numerology chart. We sow, we reap and we cannot reap what we do not sow. Indeed, our numbers of this life tell the story, in part, of our actions from past lives.

A SIMPLE NUMEROLOGY PROJECT

It is easy to prove this for yourself. What you're going to do, if you choose, is calculate your simple Lifepath number, which represents the lessons, influences, subjects and themes (LIST) confronting you in this lifetime, in this incarnation. Just follow along. It's an easy process.

Write down the day, month and year of your birth using a single number format. Add the numbers together from left to right and reduce to a single digit if necessary. For example, a birthdate of 5 December 1993 would look like this (December is the 12th month):

$$5 + 1 + 2 + 1 + 9 + 9 + 3 = 30: 3 + 0 = 3$$

The Lifepath is 3.

Another example: 27 April (the 4th month) 2018.

$$2 + 7 + 4 + 2 + 0 + 1 + 8 = 24: 2 + 4 = 6.$$

The Lifepath is 6.

Very simple, right? The next step is to calculate your own Simple Lifepath number. Correlate that single number of your Lifepath with the Lifepath Descriptions which follow. You will notice a direct correlation between that number and the lessons, issues, subjects and themes (LIST) of your life. Please note, however, this is a simple process giving simple results. A full King's Numerology™ chart delves deeply into the destiny and is much more thorough. Still, correlating your Lifepath (LP) number with your life's experiences will reveal your personal connection between numbers and life and get you started on realizing the veracity of numerology as a science. Here's the simple formula:

Day of birth + Month of birth + Year of birth = Lifepath

SIMPLE LIFEPATH DESCRIPTIONS

NOTE: The following information, with modifications, is from Chapter Eight of *The King's Book of Numerology, Volume 1 – Foundations & Fundamentals.* As of 2019, there are twelve volumes in *The King's Book of Numerology™* series. All of Richard Andrew King's books are available at RichardKing.net/books and Amazon.com.

1 Lifepath

Lessons are of the self, the yang, independence, standing on one's own two feet and not leaning on others, self-reliance, self-confidence, individuality, starts, beginnings, leadership, pioneering, assertiveness and ego. On a spiritual level, they are about Oneness, atonement, and union with the Divine. The One is the one who is detached and alone, the one who stands apart from the crowd, the one who marches to the beat of his own drum, who goes first and shows the way, who is unique, active, assertive, original, masculine, dominant, self-directed and filled with purpose. One is fire; it is also the magician. The One Lifepath is not about following others or being supported by others. It is about being out front, leading, directing and making one's way for oneself.

Notes:

2 Lifepath

Two is the vibration of partnership, relationship, dependence, support, femininity, passivity, receptivity and water - attributes quite contradictory to the number One. The 2 vibration represents the duality of the cosmos, the yin and yang, masculine and feminine, positive and negative.

A pure 2 Lifepath is one of support, service, receptivity, partnership, relationship, cooperation, togetherness, femininity, passivity, balance, harmony, caring, teamwork. The 2 Lifepath will bring conditions into the life which allow for, in fact create, support roles where the helper or helpmate assists another or others.

The 2 Lifepath also represents opposition, confliction, competition, adversity, adversaries, duplicity, deceit, duality, diplomacy, negotiation, harmony and inharmony, war and peace - both sides of its energetic structure.

In contrast to the 1 LifePath of independence, the 2 Lifepath mirrors more dependent roles and lessons. Its power lies in being the "power behind the throne," not the one sitting on the throne.

Notes:

3 Lifepath

The Three Lifepath involves lessons and themes of personal expression and integration, health, beauty, communication, friends, marriage, art, music, singing, writing, fun, pleasure and general good times. Of the nine basic numbers, the 3 generally gives the easiest life lessons when not negatively aspected.

The 3 vibration focuses on the principle of the triad in varying aspects: Father-Son-Holy Ghost; Master-Disciple-Word; Body-Mind-Spirit; Husband-Wife-Child. When a 3 is in the Lifepath, it doesn't necessarily mean life will be rosy. It means the one who possesses this script will be learning about the attributes of the 3 energy.

The 3 Lifepath will cause an individual to be involved in all areas that involve communication, beauty, pleasure, health and well-being. Actors, singers, writers, reporters, models, authors, artists, medical personnel, the media, etc., may share a 3 Lifepath.

Entitlement, narcissism, vanity and ease of living could easily be factors for a 3 Lifepath. Care should be exercised in overt pleasure-seeking involving alcohol, drugs and sex.

Notes:

4 Lifepath

Four is the first earth sign. Its lifepath represents those lessons which address that which is grounded, rooted, traditional, conventional, conservative, practical, disciplined, controlled, effort-filled, effort-compelled and service oriented. Individuals with a 4 Lifepath will experience work and effort, possibly toil, and learn lessons associated with rules, order, organization, development, structure, stability and security of all kinds - physical, emotional, social, psychological, financial, spiritual.

Four is represented by the square, the box, which can serve as something to stand on, be locked within or chained to as an anchor or lodestone. It is rigid and extremely delineated. Under this vibration, one may experience comfort or confinement depending on how it is aspected with other numerological vibrations. The Four does not generally flow, create or originate as the 1 or 3 would. It works, serves, toils and plods. Four sinks roots, clings and loves to lead the life of the immovable rock, not the rolling stone. Do not look for much diversity or adventure with the 4 Lifepath. It is very grounded, even stubborn and resistant, sometimes to a fault.

Notes:

5 Lifepath

Five encompasses the winds of change - constant, relentless, ceaseless motion; movement which can be as exasperating as it is stimulating. Because of its changing nature, 5 brings experience and freedom to one's life. Five is definitely active, filled with fire and uncertainty. The only roots 5 has are in the wind, but there is a constancy in its changing nature which brings with it the comfort and warmth of changeless change. A 5 Lifepath, therefore, is never boring, dull or lackluster. The 5 brings excitement, adventure and exploration to a person's life.

While the spiritual lesson of the 4 Lifepath is discipline and self-control, the spiritual lesson of the 5 is detachment. The 5 Lifepath forces souls not to cling, not to become too attached to things, people, events, circumstances, conditions and philosophies. It does this by moving the soul constantly from place to place - physically, mentally, emotionally, geographically, financially, spiritually.

Five loves variety because variety is a manifestation of change. Through variety, nothing is the same and cannot, therefore, be boring. Five rules the senses, of which there are five, and herein lies one of its greatest challenges. People with the 5 Lifepath may indulge themselves too much in binding, sensual experiences involving drugs, sex and risky behaviors because, after all, the 5 wants to explore and experience life. The 5 governs speed and unchecked speed can lead to trouble and problems.

Another issue for the 5 is freedom. The individual with the 5 Lifepath must learn that freedom is not license - unrestricted action without consequence - but, rather, that freedom is unrestricted action with consequence. True freedom is not obtained as a result of the absence of rules but, in fact, strict adherence to them.

Freedom is rooted in action. Unrestricted action without consequence does not exist. Karmic Law is inviolate and ceaseless in this domain. What we do, all that we do, returns to us full circle in time and there is absolutely no avoiding or escaping our actions. Because 5 loves freedom and non-restriction, it must move and act cautiously, wisely and responsibly because the consequences of such freedom may not bring freedom at all but, rather, the pain-bearing tears of enslavement and damnation.

Notes:

6 Lifepath

Heart, hearth, home, personal love, domesticity, duty, community, adjustments, nurturing, responsibility. These are characteristics of the 6 Lifepath. An individual transiting this 6 Lifepath will be involved in all that involves "ticker" - the beating of the heart - from romance to relatives, home and community.

Six, a higher octave of the 2, is the warmest and most loving of all the basic numbers. Positively expressed, it reflects that which is soft, sweet, tender, gentle, kind, caring, tolerant, patient, nurturing, supportive and harmonizing. The 6 energy demonstrates these qualities primarily in the home environment.

In the 6 Lifepath one will generally learn to make others happy, do for them, support them, love and care for them, nurture them. In its highest expression, the 6 Lifepath radiates unconditional personal love.

This 6 Lifepath also includes music. Many musicians and singers have 6 dominant in their charts. Beauty and art are also aspects the 6, especially that beauty which is loving and harmonious, sweetly flowing and warmly pleasing. On its negative side, the 6 Lifepath may manifest jealousy, envy, resentment, dislike, even hatred.

Notes:

7 Lifepath

The 7 Lifepath is the royal highway to spirituality. It is the vein that does not lead to gold but to Light. It is the doorway to the inner worlds. It moves one from a consciousness of reality to Reality.

There is no other vibration more potent for quickening the spirit than the 7 Lifepath. It does not make a man monetarily rich. Rather, it makes a man enlightened. Those who follow this path are possibly in for, not the ride of their lives, but the ride of their existence.

However, as grand, noble and spiritual as the 7 Lifepath can be, it does not come without a price. The price is often pain, tragedy, heartache, heartbreak, agony, loneliness, betrayal, ignominy, dishonor, long-suffering, extreme frustration and misfortune. As Perfect Master Maharaj Charan Singh Ji has stated: "For getting the highest thing in life, we have to pay the highest price." The cost of moving into the inner worlds is the release, the giving up, the letting go of the outer worlds and all they represent and reflect.

In order to begin this inner quest of the spirit, we must be detached from that which is material. This is difficult for most of us because we have been transiting the outer worlds of flesh and form for eons in countless incarnations, and our consciousness has grown accustomed to the External Illusion to such a degree that we resemble barnacles stuck to the wet, storm-worn, weather-washed rock walls of the material monolith we call earthly existence.

However, to follow the inner path, we must be pried free of our tenacious attachment and carnal cohesion. So, along comes the 7 energy to sever these binding bonds by giving us solitude to reflect on life, isolation to protect us from the insidious nature of others, heartache and heartbreak to move us away from worldly loves to Divine love, betrayal to cut the ties to those to whom we cling, ignominy and dishonor to teach us humility, disease to teach us patience and tranquillity and long-suffering to make us wait . . . and burn . . . and become pure.

Unfortunately, many souls who are living the 7 Lifepath miss the point. Rather than turn inward to find the way out – for the way out is in – they continue to run out, seeking solace for their problems by clinging harder to the very rock which anchors them to this nether land and from which they must break away to be free.

Alcoholism is one way some souls choose to find peace from the detaching turmoil of their existence. They drown their suffering in liquid poison, which only further poisons their lives and, ultimately, leads to additional pain and suffering. Recreational drug addiction and illicit love relationships are also false avenues to peace.

However, there comes a time in the development of the spiritual self when it must learn to be patient and endure its suffering, not attempt to mask it or run away from it, because it is the suffering that purifies and purity is the essential essence of the Spirit.

To be one with the Spirit, one must be pure and to be pure, most of us must endure the fires of purification which suffering brings. In its highest purpose, life is not about comfort. It is about God Realization, and it is no easy thing to make the transition from a worldly-centered life to a God-centered one. But . . . if we're to achieve our liberation, it must be done. Hence, the soul is graced with the energy of the 7 Lifepath and its characteristics of isolation, patience, tolerance, calmness, quietude, reclusiveness, separation, suffering, tragedy, misfortune, chaos and calamity to assist us in our divine quest.

In social gatherings, when others are mixing and interacting, it is the 7 which stands or sits off to the side – alone, quiet, pensive, seemingly distant and cool. Seven is not a social mixer. It is an internal dweller. It thinks, reflects, cogitates, meditates, muses, observes, questions and analyzes. For externally focused souls, it may be "hip and happening" to be socially gregarious, but for the indwelling 7, it's all happening on the inside, and socializing is as dull and boring to it as the inner existence is to those seeking social interaction (8 Lifepath).

Sometimes, being and feeling alone and separated from others may cause worry and concern. One should not worry but understand the 7's purpose, which is to be separate from the "outer life" in order to embrace the "inner life" and its divine purpose. The way out is in, and it is "In" where we find the true purpose of life. Although the 7 Lifepath is difficult, it is *the doorway* to eternal Truth. It must not, therefore, be feared but embraced and lived.

Notes:

8 Lifepath

The 8 Lifepath is the script of interaction, connection, disconnection, engagement, commerce, management and all that is involved in the principle of "flow."

The 8 Lifepath energy connects polarities – male to female; buyer to seller; concept to completion; management to labor; product to consumer; past to present. In contrast to the 7 Lifepath and its internal energies, the 8 Lifepath is focused on external energies, socialization, worldliness, comfort and status.

Those souls who travel the 8 Lifepath will be compelled to focus their attention generally on external, social, worldly, material matters. But not always. There are exceptions to every rule. As every number has a positive and negative polarity, so does it have a spiritual and material aspect as well. Eight can be a very spiritual number, seeking to make a connection between God and man, the inner worlds and outer worlds. But, generally, in this dimension, 8 energy can be thought of as worldly.

Those who have an 8 Lifepath can make very good executives, managers, leaders and administrators because the specific function of these positions demands a coordination of all parts of the whole. From top to bottom, low rung to high rung, basement to penthouse, janitor to president, the leader is the one who insures that all is flowing efficiently, smoothly, properly and, hopefully, fairly, humanely and lovingly to insure that the whole organization or institution is successful. And let it be said that the most successful of these individuals will be the ones who see themselves as servants – not bosses, big shots or rulers. The positive 8 works with others to achieve an efficient and harmonious flow within the structure of the organization it serves. And that is the operative word – serve, for the positive 8 serves, not subjugates.

High level athletes and performers often carry this 8 cipher in their Lifepath. Athletes must be coordinated, and it is the 8 energy that creates a condition of coordination. Having the ability to get the ball in the hoop, the pass to the receiver, the puck in the net, the kick to the target, the parry to the punch, the car to the finish line, the skis over the moguls, the feeling of the song or the meaning of the message to the audience and so forth is all a matter of coordination – the natural function of the 8.

The 8 energy seeks success or, what is traditionally regarded as success – wealth, social status, power, recognition, fame, authority and possessions. The non-traditional 8 seeks success in terms of a connection with a higher Power. Regardless of the focus, they both want to make that connection which integrates the flow of an idea, impulse or desire with its manifestation, yielding that state of being or accomplishment we regard as success.

Although 8 integrates, administrates and coordinates, it can also manipulate. Eight governs flow. It doesn't govern purity, ethics or morality. It simply moves between polarities making connections or disconnections. As money moves through all types of hands, so the 8 energy moves through and between all types of people with all types of motives and intentions. It is only when operating within the sphere of a spiritually elevated consciousness that we can trust the 8's goodness, sincerity, purpose and truthfulness.

Notes:

9 Lifepath

The 9 Lifepath focuses on the macrocosm, the big picture, the universal stage, travel and rulership. In contrast to the personal loving vibration of the 6, the 9 represents impersonal love. It manifests as compassion, caring, concern, involvement and service in the arena of the 'many', the masses, the public.

The 9 energy reflects the humanitarian, philanthropist, philosopher, teacher, doctor, nurse, singer, actor, writer, thespian, theologian, performer - basically any occupation associated with the public in general. The 9's energy of universality makes it both magnetic and charismatic.

Because of its universal appeal, the 9 Lifepath often brings public recognition, fame, fortune and travel, often on a global scale. In spite of how popular the individual with the 9 Lifepath may or may not be, it is certain that he or she will be involved with the public and the mass of humanity in some way. An individual may even be cast into the limelight. What happens when he gets there is another issue.

The 9 Lifepath often leads one into the profession of music and its performance. No one needs words to understand music because music is universally felt and experienced - an aspect of the 9 vibration.

The 9 energy also rules endings, conclusions, completions and terminations. Thus, one with a 9 Lifepath may find himself involved with many endings and finalizations in life. Perhaps one will even complete a project in this lifetime begun lifetimes earlier in another incarnation. Who knows? Because life is a continuum and reincarnation a reality, such an idea is plausible.

The main lesson for one with the 9 Lifepath is to be involved with the 'many', the masses, the public. Serve, perform, rule, but do so with great care, responsibility and caution. Karma is never not working in this creation. Great actions bear great reactions and when one is spotlighted on the great stage of life, the consequences can be critical to one's evolution.

So what is your Lifepath number? It should make sense to you. It is part of your destiny and a manifestation of your karma in this incarnation.

Notes:

THE NUMEROLOGY OF KARMA

The numerology of the word "Karma" could not be more perfect. Its Specific Expression (Expression = the word itself) is the Master number 44. Its General Expression is an 8 (the 44 in reduction: 4 + 4 = 8). The full ciphering of the word Karma, therefore, is 44-8.

In numerology every letter has two numeric values based on the English alphabet and its twenty-six letters – a Specific value and a General value. The Specific value is the actual number of its placement in the alphabet. For example, the letter "A" has a Specific value of 1 because it's the first letter of the alphabet; the letter "Z" has a Specific value of 26 because it's the twenty-sixth letter of the alphabet. The ampersand ("&") is actually the twenty-seventh letter of the English alphabet and has a value of 9.

Therefore, adding the Specific values of each letter of the word "Karma" generates the 44 Master number:

K (11) + A (1) + R (18) + M (13) + A (1) = 44

Reducing the 44 to a single digit, the 8 appears (4 + 4 = 8), which is the General Expression for the word "Karma."

As we know, the process of karma is to return the action of the doer to himself, completing the cycle of action and reaction. This is exactly the function of the 8 energy, i.e., connecting action and reaction or, in other words, completing the circuit of cause and consequence, sowing and reaping.

The 44 Specific Expression is the dual cipher master root of the 8. The number 4 in numerology is associated with rules, order, organization, constructing, building, designing and creating form and structure. Karma is the invisible manifestation of the process of completing the sowing and reaping cycle.

The 44-8 Master energy is associated with generals, CEOs, managers, leaders, organizers. These are the people who connect the varied parts of an organization, team, army and company together to generate flow and efficiency.

Many leaders have the 44-8 in their charts. Thomas Jefferson, General Douglas MacArthur, General George Patton, Ulysses S. Grant, Helen Keller and Mother Teresa all have the 44-8 in their charts. For this reason The King's Numerology™ refers to the 44-8 as the "Generalship" energy.

How beautiful then is the word "Karma" related to its numeric function? It is perfect. The 44-8 is the most powerful numeric energy of organization in numerology, and Karmic Law is the absolute process of maintaining order in this creation. It could not be more perfect.

To learn more about numerology, the twelve volumes of *The King's Book of Numerology*tm series (TKBN) are available at RichardKing.net/books, Amazon.com, and other booksellers.

***The King's Book of Numerology*tm – Volume Titles**

Note: Reference to a "Stand Alone Book" indicates that it is not necessary to have read previous volumes of the *The King's Book of Numerology*tm series to understand it. Hence, the meaning of a "Stand Alone Book."

TKBN Volume 1: *Foundations & Fundamentals*

TKBN Volume 2: *Forecasting, Part 1*

TKBN Volume 3: *Master Numbers*

TKBN Volume 4: *Intermediate Principles*

TKBN Volume 5: *I/R Sets, Level 1* (I/R = Influence/Reality)

TKBN Volume 6: *Love Relationships* (a "stand alone book")

TKBN Volume 7: *Parenting Wisdom* (a "stand alone book")

TKBN Volume 8: *Forecasting, Part 2*

TKBN Volume 9: *Numeric Biography – Princess Diana* (a "stand alone book")

TKBN Volume 10: *Historic Icons, Part 1*(a "stand alone book")

TKBN Volume 11: *The Age of the Female – Volumes 1 & 2* (a "stand alone book")

TKBN Volume 12: *Advanced Principles*

NUMBER POWER

Numbers tell the time;
as well, they tell the tale;
numbers calculate the voyage
of life in its detail.

Numbers, just like coins,
incorporate two sides –
positive and negative,
as in the turn of tides.

Numbers are the codes of life;
they gauge, describe, define
the framework and the structure
of a life that is divine.

Numbers are life's basis
and, as cosmic law avers,
the blueprint of our destiny
has its design in numbers.

RICHARD ANDREW KING
~ Books ~

RichardKing.net, Amazon.com and Major Online Retailers

The King's Book of Numerology
(KBN1)
Volume 1-Foundations & Fundamentals

The King's Book of Numerology, Volume 1-Foundations & Fundamentals provides complete descriptions of Basic Numbers, Double Numbers, Purifier Numbers, Master Numbers, the Letters in Simple and Specific form as well as the Basic Matrix, the numerological blueprint of our lives.

The King's Book of Numerology™ series contains new information that informs and predicts more completely and accurately than any previously published numerological work. It brings back the empowered sciences of long ago, information long since lost upon this plane. ~ G. Shaver

The best numerology book I've ever read. ~ M.W.

I've learned as much about numerology from 'The King's Book of Numerology' the last few days than I have in my past five years of study.
~ Frank M

The King's Book of Numerology II (KBN2)

Forecasting – Part 1

The King's Book of Numerology II: Forecasting – Part 1 is dedicated to opening the door to the divine blueprint of our lives. That plan, that divine blueprint of destiny, is exact, precise, unchangeable, unalterable and . . . knowable, at least in general terms.

Once this awareness of a predetermined fate becomes established through application of numbers and their truths, our understanding and consciousness of life will, no doubt, change. We will begin to see ourselves as part of an immense spiritual superstructure far beyond our current ability to comprehend, understand or perceive. Life will take on new meaning and, perhaps, we will even begin to awaken to greater spiritual truths. Subjects covered: Life Cycle Patterns, The Pinnacle/Challenge Matrix, Epoch Timeline, Voids, Case Studies and much more.

The King's Book of Numerology 3
(KBN3)
Master Numbers

The King's Book of Numerology 3 – Master Numbers delves deeply into the subject of master numbers – multiple digit numbers of the same cipher, focusing especially on binary master numbers: 11-22-33-44-55-66-77-88-99.

Master numbers are the nuclear component of the numeric spectrum and play powerful roles in the destinies of individuals. They cannot be ignored.

KBN3 reveals the process of discovering hidden master numbers in all facets of a King's Numerology^{tm} chart, how voids effect the life and much more.

Richard Andrew King

The King's Book of Numerology 4
(KBN4)

Intermediate Principles

The King's Book of Numerology 4 – Intermediate Principles will expand your consciousness of the mysteries of life and destiny by taking you deeper into the secret world of numbers and their meaning.

Life is energy. People are energy. Numbers are arithmetic codes describing and defining the energies that comprise our lives and destinies. Like priceless treasures discovered during an archaeological dig, numbers and number patterns buried beneath the surface of single numbers contain a treasure trove of untold wealth and secret riches of knowledge and wisdom.

Intermediate Principles chapters include Common Names, Linkage, Stacking, Name Suffixes, Binary Capsets, Influence/Reality Set Formats, Dual Basic Matrix Components, Subcap Challenges, and much more.

The King's Book of Numerology 5
(KBN5)

I/R Sets – Level 1

IR SETS are the crux, core and substance of numerology forecasting, indispensable to the King's Numerology[tm] system and to anyone choosing to know where they've been, where they are now and where they're headed. They are obligatory for any serious and professional numerologist.

The King's Book of Numerology 5: I/R Sets – Level 1 offers a general explanation of each of the 81 IR Sets in order to create a foundation on which to build a greater understanding of how life's events affect us. KBN5 is a starting point from which to grow greater knowledge of one's self and destiny.

IR SETS are a gift for those willing to receive them, study them and apply their vast level of knowledge to make our lives more understandable, manageable, easier, better, whole.

Richard Andrew King

The King's Book of Numerology 6
(KBN6)

Love Relationships (Stand alone)

Note: This is a "stand alone" book. Its knowledge is not dependent on prior KBN publications.

The King's Book of Numerology, Volume 6 – Love Relationships (KBN6) guides you through this revolutionary method of understanding the Secrets of Love and Happiness via the mystical science of numbers. If you can add 1 + 1, you can quickly learn how to utilize and benefit from the great truths shared within this book.

The fundamental Secret of all great relationships, marriages and partnerships revolves around the quality and quantity of Mutual Energetic Resonance between the partners. This resonance (MER) is easily identified from the natal data of the individuals involved – their full birth names and birth dates. In fact, this birth data is where the mysteries of everything, including love relationships and destiny, all begins.

KBN6 is divided into two parts: Part 1 is the original book Your Love Numbers; Part 2 puts the King's Numerologytm number science to the test with twenty marital case studies broken into three segments: Section I. Marriages rated as excellent; Section II. Celebrity marriages ending in divorce; and Section III. Hollywood marriages that have endured. These case studies are powerfully insightful because they reveal, without question, the dramatic and irrefutable correlation between love and numbers.

The King's Book of Numerology 7
(KBN7)

Parenting Wisdom (Stand alone)

The King's Book of Numerology, Volume 7: Parenting Wisdom – Numerology & Life Truths (KBN7) is a compilation of two books in one. The reason for this is twofold: 1. To place the *Parenting Wisdom* series in one convenient resource; 2. As a continuing effort to place all King's Numerology^tm books under one banner. KBN7 is also a "stand alone" book. Its knowledge is not dependent on having read prior KBN publications.

KBN7-Part 1: *Parenting Wisdom for the 21st Century – Raising Your Children by Their Numbers to Achieve Their Highest Potential* reveals the secrets to understanding a child's Basic Matrix and destiny through the most ancient of all sciences, numbers. Using numerology to help raise children is a revolutionary idea, reaping great rewards for children in helping them understand themselves, their life's journey and destiny.

KBN7-Part 2: *Parenting Wisdom – What to Teach the Children* offers thirty-three time-tested universal principles of life which parents can use to create a strong foundation for their children, allowing them to develop into whole, fulfilled and substantive adults. These thirty-three fundamental concepts offer parents a road map and paradigm of what to teach the children.

The King's Book of Numerology 8 (KBN8)

Forecasting, Part 2

The King's Book of Numerology, Volume 8 – Forecasting, Part 2 (KBN8) broadens and expands the knowledge of numerology forecasting into areas of greater depth and specificity, giving students and practitioners of this divine numeric science tools unknown heretofore, allowing them to rise to the zenith of understanding in decoding life and destiny, and once again proving that life is destined and that the blueprint of destiny is, indisputably, secretly hidden in our birth names and birth dates. Indeed, God did not drop us here without a plan or a way of knowing that plan if we so choose.

The King's Book of Numerology, Volume 8 – Forecasting, Part 2

Contents

The X-Y Paradigm, Cycle of Nines, Timeline Transitions, Lifetime Monthly Timeline (LMT), Annual Cycle Patterns – Monthly Timelines, Monthly Cycle Patterns (MCPs), Life Changes and the Number 5, Master Filters, Master Amalgams, Crown Roots/Pillars, Addresses – Homes and Businesses, Numerology Forecasting – Step-by-Step Analysis, and the 2016 Presidential Election Series – Articles: 1 to 10

The King's Book of Numerology 9
(KBN9)

Numeric Biography – Princess Diana

(Stand alone)

The King's Book of Numerology, Volume 9 – Numeric Biography, Princess Diana was originally published as *Blueprint of a Princess – Diana Frances Spencer, Queen of Hearts*, in 1998 and reprised in 2017 – the 20th Anniversary of Diana's death – to be included in The King's Book of Numerology Series.

KBN9 thoroughly explains the life, destiny and heartbreak of Princess Diana based on the King's Numerologytm and its system of numeric coding.

For a more thorough explanation, see the following *Blueprint of a Princess* description.

Richard Andrew King

The King's Book of Numerology 10
(KBN10)

Historic Icons – Part 1

(Stand alone)

The King's Book of Numerology, Volume 10 – Historic Icons, Part 1 (KBN10) was initially published as *Destinies of the Rich & Famous – The Secret Numbers of Extraordinary Lives* and has been added to The King's Book of Numerology^{tm} series to expand its platform.

WHY do individuals become historic icons? What is it in their numbers allowing them to be rich or successful or famous or universally known globally and historically? Is it luck? Hard work? Advantage by family name? No. It is destiny, purely and simply, and the blueprint of that destiny is contained within the full birth name and birth date of each of these featured icons.

The King's Book of Numerology11
(KBN11)

The Age of the Female - Volumes 1 & 2

(Stand alone)

The King's Book of Numerology, Volume 11 (KBN11) is a stand alone work of two books in one: *The Age of the Female - A Thousand Years of Yin* and *The Age of the Female 2 - Heroines of the Shift* (both works published separately in 2008).

The Age of the Female - A Thousand Years of Yin, corroborates the profound and extraordinary ascent of the female in the modern world and explains exactly why this 2nd Millennium belongs, not to Him (the Yang), but to Her (the Yin). It is an insightful, stimulating and consciousness-expanding read into this new thousand year period of time, offering compelling and irrefutable evidence through the King's Numerology^{tm} that, indeed, the Age of the Female has arrived.

The Age of the Female 2 - Heroines of the Shift is not numerologically based. Rather, it continues the remarkable journey of the female's ascent in the 20th Century by honoring Her accomplishments in the categories of: Female Firsts, Female Nobel Laureates, Female Athletes, Female Icons and Female Quotations. These chapters are a rich source of inspiration, serving as a catalyst for every individual (male or female) to be the best he or she can be and to honor the very essence of what it is to be human.

"The Age of the Female" by Richard Andrew King is an affirming, guiding light, and "The Age of the Female II: Heroines of the Shift" - what fabulously inspiring company!

~ LaVerne Baker Hotep

The King's Book of Numerology12
(KBN12)
Advanced Principles

The King's Book of Numerology, Volume 12 – Advanced Principles (KBN12) offers seasoned King's Numerology™ followers further insights, knowledge and understanding into the divine science of numeric coding, allowing for the expansion of human consciousness beyond the mundane world of phenomena to the mystical world of Divine Reality.

Chapters in KBN12 are:

1. The Numerology of Dislike
2. The Numerology of Betrayal
3. Nemesis Numbers
4. Common Name Dynamics
5. Single Name Analysis Profile – SNAP
6. Numerology of Past Lives
7. Family Ties
8. Life Journey Shifts and Changes
9. Voids, Vacuums and Karmic Scales
10. The Life Matrix Diamond
11. Professional Chart Analysis
12. The King's Book of Numerology™
    Series Summation-Volumes 1 through 12

Blueprint of a Princess

Diana Frances Spencer - Queen of Hearts

The tragic death of Princess Diana of Wales - the most famous, the most photographed, the most written about woman of the modern world and possibly of all time - was one of the most shocking and saddening events of the late Twentieth Century. Not since the assassination of American President John Fitzgerald Kennedy in 1963, has such an event captured the attention of the world. On that ill-fated Sunday of 31 August 1997, and the following week until her funeral, there was much discussion and reflection of the Queen of Hearts, the People's Princess, England's Rose. But in all of the media news coverage, there was no discussion given to the cosmic aspects of her life and death.

Blueprint of a Princess is dedicated to addressing those issues through The King's Numerologytm. Its purpose and hope is to offer some consolation and explanation as to that one question so poignantly written on a card of condolence left with the multitude of flowers before the gates of Buckingham Palace. . . "Why?"

After learning from King's numerological teaching, it is impossible to conceive of going back to that 'twilight naive and foggy' state of being where one can only guess or hint at the truths, motivations and directions of one's life that are Pre-King. Not only do I recommend this book, but I suggest it and his other numerology books as absolutely necessary for the library of anyone even remotely interested in the science of numerology. ~
Hunter Stowers

99 Poems of the Spirit

99 Poems of the Spirit draws from the writings of Perfect Saints, Masters, Mystics and Sacred Scriptures. Designed to lift the consciousness, mind and heart, all of the poems are original works by Richard Andrew King. Their purpose is to help connect the reader with the mystic side of life in order to enhance the process of self-realization while advancing on the spiritual path and climbing the ladder leading to the ultimate attainment of God Realization. It is a treasure chest of poetic spiritual gems offered to excite, educate and stimulate the mind and soul in the glorious journey of spiritual ascent.

Messages from the Masters

Timeless Truths for Spiritual Seekers

In a time where there is more need for enlightenment than ever before, Messages from the Masters: Timeless Truths for Spiritual Seekers offers timeless truths for genuine seekers thirsty for spiritual nectar.

Masters are the PhDs of the universe, the Light Bearers of the Divine Flame. Their knowledge and wisdom are supreme. They have no equal. Although appearing human, they are not. Masters are the exalted Sons of God. Their chief duty is to rescue souls, liberating them from the maniacal maelstrom and madness of the material world and returning them to their eternal Home with the Lord.

Messages from the Masters is a rich source of hundreds of quotes from a cavalcade of nine Perfect Saints throughout the last six hundred years: Guru Ravidas, Kabir, Guru Nanak, Tulsi Sahib, Swami Ji Maharaj, Baba Jaimal Singh, Sawan Singh, Jagat Singh and Charan Singh. The messages in this book focus on the importance of the Divine Diet, the priceless Human Form, Reincarnation, the World, the Negative Power and Soul Food.
Warning! Messages from the Masters is not for the faint of heart or the worldly-minded. Masters come into the world to sever our attachment to it, not make it a paradise. Although the epitome of love and wisdom, they shoot straight from the hip, pull no punches, favor no religion. Their universal message of soul liberation is reflected in the statement of Saint Maharaj Charan Singh: Just live in the creation and get out of it!

The Age of the Female

A Thousand Years of Yin

The Age of the Female: A Thousand Years of Yin highlights the profound and extraordinary ascent of the female in the modern world, placing her center stage in the global spotlight as presidents and leaders of nations, titans of industry, corporate executives, military generals, media magnets, doctors, lawyers and a whole host of other prestigious titles normally associated with the male. Why has her rise to prominence been so rapid, especially in consideration of historic time? Why also has there been an increased interest in other people's lives in our society, in competitive athletics, personal data collection and the exploration of space and other worlds? *The Age of the Female: A Thousand Years of Yin* answers these questions. It is an insightful and exciting read into these mysteries, offering compelling and irrefutable evidence through the ancient science and art of numerology that, indeed, the age of the female has arrived and the next thousand years belong, not to him, but to her.

The Age of the Female II

Heroines of the Shift

The Age of the Female II: Heroines of the Shift continues the remarkable journey of the female's ascent in the modern world of the 2nd Millennium. This installment is a general read in five chapters honoring the accomplishments of women in categories of female firsts, female Nobel laureates, female athletes, female icons and female quotations.

The achievements of the women featured in *The Age of the Female II: Heroines of the Shift* are deserving of respect and admiration. Their lives, challenges and successes are motivational catalysts for every individual to be the best he or she can be and to honor the very essence of what it is to be human. *The Age of the Female II: Heroines of the Shift* is intended to be an inspiring and educational read for everyone, not just women but men, too, offering knowledge and insight of the depth, power and daring-do of women as their Yin energy rises upon the global stage in this millennium which destiny has irrefutably marked as the Age of the Female.

Richard Andrew King

Your Love Numbers

Discovering the Secrets of Your Life, Loves and Relationships

Your Love Numbers reveals the secret formula defining all great relationships and how to assess the love potential of any relationship in a matter of minutes.

Your Love Numbers teaches you how to assess a relationship or potential relationship in minutes, saving you endless time, energy, effort and possible heartache in the end. By knowing ourselves and the people we love, our relationships will be potentially more rewarding, satisfying, productive, peaceful, lasting and loving . . . for everyone - our family, spouses, partners, children, friends.

Your Love Numbers explains the mystery of love through the most ancient of all sciences . . . numbers, your numbers, calculated using only your full name and date of birth and those of the people you love! "Numbers rule the universe; everything is arranged according to number and mathematical shape," said Pythagoras. Everything - including light, sound and love can be measured in numbers! *Your Love Numbers* is based on thirty years of relationship research by master numerologist, Richard Andrew King. Applying his unique and revolutionary new theories, love and attraction between people can be determined using very easy to learn concepts. With a little study and practice, all this can be done in a minutes.

The Galactic Transcripts

The Galactic Transcripts will take you on a journey that is as provocative as it is mysterious. Its thirty-seven transmissions are channeled from a non-earth, alien group who identify themselves as members of the Space Brotherhood.

The Galactic Transcripts offer us descriptions of other worlds, their inhabitants, morals, ethics, and histories. They even forewarn of the coming cleansing of earth and the cataclysms preceding it. Other messages shed light on the original colonization of earth, telepathic communication, the power of love, the program of the Radiant One, and much more.

Those who have read *The Galactic Transcripts* have found them to be life-altering, profound, inspirational, transformative. Will they have that effect on you? Open your mind and allow the transcripts to take you beyond the limitations of our world and into new, undiscovered worlds far beyond our galaxy.

RichardKing.net
TheGalacticTranscripts.com

Richard Andrew King

The Black Belt Book of Life

Secrets of a Martial Arts Master

The mystery and mystique of the martial arts is not only ages old, it's legend. Revered throughout the world, martial arts is a treasure chest of life secrets that transcend the boundaries of combat to include the expanse of life and living. Arguably, it is the greatest developmental system on earth for teaching the integration of body, mind and spirit

The Black Belt Book of Life: Secrets of a Martial Arts Master is not about physical fighting strategies and tactics. It is about concepts and principles we learn though martial arts training that can help us in the struggle of life, in the journey to conquer ourselves and gain the golden ring of our own completeness because in the end a true Black Belt should be a realized soul who, having engaged the enemy - himself - finds himself at the end of the journey, triumphant.

The Black Belt Book of Life: Secrets of a Martial Arts Master reveals many secrets of martial arts training, sharing these truths in quick and easy to read vignettes to benefit martial artists and the general public as well. It is a book for all readers, not just martial artists, both males and females, especially the youth of today who are in search of a foundation to guide their lives.

The Karate Consciousness

From Worldly Warrior to Mystic Master

The Karate Consciousness – From Worldly Warrior to Mystic Master is dedicated to the philosophy that karate is both an excellent system for the integration of body, mind and spirit as well as an excellent vehicle for the evolution of one's consciousness of life from a mundane perspective to a more elevated and edified reality.

Just as many martial arts systems are comprised of an ascending ladder of colored belts to designate accomplishment, so life is also comprised of an ascending ladder of levels of consciousness from worldly to divine.

The Karate Consciousness – From Worldly Warrior to Mystic Master shares concepts and perspectives which may help the karate practitioner in climbing the "Ladder of Consciousness." Among such concepts are the Power in the Flock Syndrome, the Continuum, the D.C. Factor, the Great Law of Karma and much more.

Richard Andrew King

Destinies of the Rich & Famous

The Secret Numbers of Extraordinary Lives

Why are rich and famous people rich and famous? Is it luck? Hard work? Advantage by family name? What makes them special? What secrets are the basis of their success?

Destinies of the Rich & Famous explores the secret numbers of the following famous global icons and explains through The King's Numerology[tm] why they are both rich and famous - Dr. Albert Einstein, Amelia Earhart, Elvis Presley, General George Patton, Howard Hughes, John F. Kennedy, Marilyn Monroe, Michael Jackson, Muhammad Ali, Oprah Winfrey, Princess Diana and Sarah Palin.

Destinies of the Rich & Famous answers these questions and much more. Too, it reveals the clear correlation between a person's life and his or her natal data - the date of birth and full name of birth, illustrating the reality that fame and fortune and destined!

Parenting Wisdom

Raising Your Children By Their Numbers
To Achieve Their Highest Potential

This book is a must for any parent and all parents to be. It is vital to read this book now before you name your children. If you already have children, then it is just as important to understand them.

Richard Andrew King should be called Dr. King. His books are of the magnitude that will be read with reverence for generations to come. ~ Dr. Victoria Ford, J.D.

Parenting Wisdom for the 21st Century - Raising Your Children by Their Numbers to Achieve Their Highest Potential is a revolutionary addition to the process of arguably the most important job in the world, parenting.

The powerful information contained within this work will reveal the hidden desires driving your children, the paths they will follow in life, the roles they will give on the great life stage and much more – all designed to augment your parenting wisdom and support life's paramount parental purpose . . . to love the children and help them achieve their highest potential.

ParentingWisdom.net

Parenting Wisdom 2

What To Teach The Children

This work is a companion book to *Parenting Wisdom For The 21st Century – Raising Your Children By Their Numbers To Achieve Their Highest Potential.*

Parenting is the most important and critical job in life because it encompasses the cultivating and sculpting of life itself as reflected in our children – the sanctity of life in manifest form.

In the process of parenting one of the most germane questions is, "What do we teach the children?" Parenting Wisdom offers thirty-three time-tested, universal principles which parents can use to create a strong foundation allowing children to develop into whole, fulfilled, and substantive adults.

The thirty-three principles include: The Five Needs of Children, Boundaries, Rules, And Regs, Your Life, Your Responsibility, Tender Love Versus Tough Love, The Four Cornerstones of a Substantive Life, The Temptations of S.A.D. (Sex, Alcohol, Drugs)
and much more . . .

ParentingWisdom.net

27 Delusions of Mankind

Everyone is lost in the world of delusion.
~ Saint Namdev, 13th Century

The whole world is overpowered by delusion.
The delusion is overpowered by none.
~Saint Dariya of Bihar, 17th/18th Century

Delusions are false beliefs held to be true. By subscribing to them we become more ignorant and blind to Reality than we already are. How can we be enlightened living in a cave devoid of light? We can't. That's why it is imperative for us to dissolve the delusions that entrap us, enslave us—from cradle to grave—in a prison of ignorance, keeping us from being free and whole.

The following fourteen delusions give a glimpse of some of the false beliefs plaguing humanity. *27 Delusions of Mankind* shares thirteen more. Some of these delusions may shock you; some comfort you; some will give you pause to stop and think about life, but all will open your eyes to the false beliefs we have held to be true but which, in fact, are false and need to be dissolved if we're ever to rise into the Light of our Divine Heritage.

RICHARD ANDREW KING ~ CDs

RichardKing.net, CDBaby.com, and Online Retailers

Priceless Poetry & Prose 1

Dramatizations of Famous Literary Works

Wonderfully entertaining and educational artistic dramatizations of famous literary works for adults, children, teachers and students alike. Enjoy the timeless words of Shakespeare, Lincoln, Tennyson, Longfellow, Patrick Henry, Emily Dickinson, Chaucer and more.

Priceless Poetry & Prose 2

Selected Works of Edgar Allan Poe

Be enveloped in the mysterious and haunted world of one of America's most loved poets, Edgar Allan Poe. Highly entertaining and educational, enjoy classic poems such as, The Raven, Annabel Lee, Ulalume, Alone, Lenore and more.

Poems of the Spirit

Selected Original Poems of Richard Andrew King

A collection of original spiritual poems designed to edify the mind and uplift the spirit. Not for the faint of heart or worldly-minded, these works reflect timeless truths from scriptures, saints and mystics throughout the ages - messages enabling the individual to break the shackles of worldly ties in quest for spiritual realization.

Echoes from the Heart

Selected Original Songs of Richard Andrew King

An original collection of twelve of Richard's tug-at-your-heart ballads, cowboy songs, patriotic tributes and spiritual tunes for your soul. A few titles are *Waiting for You, Don't Forget the Heroes, One More Broken Heart, The Promise, Rodeo Cowboy, You Can't Push the River, No Itty Bitty Cowboy* and *Catch Me When I Fall.*

ORDER INFORMATION

To order Books and CDs, go to
RichardKing.Net, Amazon.com
or major online retailers

CONTACT

Richard Andrew King
PO Box 3621
Laguna Hills, CA 92654
RichardKing.Net
Rich @ RichardKing.net

NOTES:

NOTES:

NOTES:

NOTES:

NOTES:

NOTES:

NOTES:

NOTES:

NOTES:

NOTES:

NOTES:

NOTES:

NOTES:

NOTES:

NOTES:

NOTES:

NOTES:

NOTES:

NOTES:

NOTES:

NOTES:

NOTES:

NOTES:

NOTES:

NOTES:

NOTES:

www.ingramcontent.com/pod-product-compliance
Lightning Source LLC
Chambersburg PA
CBHW060007100426
42740CB00010B/1429
9780931872006